The Midnight Experience

The *Midnight* Experience

A 30-Day Devotional and Study of Psalm 119

Elana Cole

EDEN
PUBLISHING COMPANY
www.edenpublishing.net

Copyright ©2018 Elana Cole

Published by Eden Publishing

P.O. Box 38691, Germantown, TN 38183

www.edenpublishing.net

Printed in the United States of America

2018 – First Edition

All rights reserved. Except as permitted under the U.S. Copyright Act of 1976, this publication shall not be broadcast, rewritten, distributed, or transmitted, electronically or copied, in any form, or stored in a database or retrieval system, without prior written permission from the author/publisher.

Library of Congress Cataloging-in-Publications Data

The Midnight Experience: A 30-Day Devotional and Study of Psalm 119/Elana Cole

LCCN: 2018909966

ISBN   978-0-692-16638-3 (pbk)
ISBN   978-0-692-16639-0 (ebook)

1.Cole, Elana 2. Faith 3.Christianity 4. Devotional

Unless otherwise indicated, all Scripture quotations are taken from the Holy Bible, New Living Translation, copyright © 1996, 2004, 2015 by Tyndale House Foundation. Used by permission of Tyndale House Publishers, Inc., Carol Stream, Illinois 60188. All rights reserved.

Scripture taken from The Message. Copyright © 1993, 1994, 1995, 1996, 2000, 2001, 2002. Used by permission of NavPress Publishing Group.

Scripture quotations marked HCSB are taken from the Holman Christian Standard Bible®, Copyright © 1999, 2000, 2002, 2003, 2009 by Holman Bible Publishers. Used by permission. Holman Christian Standard Bible®, Holman CSB®, and HCSB® are federally registered trademarks of Holman Bible Publishers.

Scripture taken from the New King James Version®. Copyright © 1982 by Thomas Nelson. Used by permission. All rights reserved.

THE HOLY BIBLE, NEW INTERNATIONAL VERSION®, NIV® Copyright © 1973, 1978, 1984, 2011 by Biblica, Inc.® Used by permission. All rights reserved worldwide.

All personal stories and/or references are true and names have been changed to protect the identity and privacy of each individual.

Dedicated to all those searching for God's peace through the darkness.

"I stay awake through the night, thinking about your promise."

Psalm 119:148 NLT

Table of Contents

Preface	11
Introduction	15
1. **Section I**	**23**
A Chiropractic Realignment from God	25
Day 1: Who are the Happiest Ones of All?	35
Day 2: The Rhythm of God	39
Day 3: Set Me Apart	43
Day 4: The Pressure is On	47
Day 5: The True Source of Happiness	51
Day 6 and 7: Recap and Reflection	55
The Endless Supplier	57
2. **Section II**	**63**
His Demonstration of True Love	65
Day 8: Anchored in His Love	73
Day 9: Hanging on for Dear Life	77
Day 10: Pure Devotion	81
Day 11: The Start of a Breakthrough	85
Day 12: Becoming a Vessel God can Use	89
Day 13 and 14: Recap and Reflection	93
A Serving of Healing	95
3. **Section III**	**101**
What's in the Eye of Your Storm?	103
Day 15: The Five W's of Waiting	111
Day 16: Silencing the Enemy	115
Day 17: Praise Break	119
Day 18: Declare It to Your Soul	123
Day 19: God's Power vs. Human Power	127
Day 20 and 21: Recap and Reflection	131
Confessions to the One who already Knows	133
4. **Section IV**	**139**
Speak Your Life into Existence	141
Day 22: The Time is Now	151

Day 23: Living to Tell about It		155
Day 24: He won't be Mocked		159
Day 25: Pray about Everything		163
Day 26: The Release		167
Day 27 and 28: Recap and Reflection		171
For Such a Time as This		173
5. **Section V**		**179**
Conclusion, but not the End		181
Day 29: Truly Transformed Forever		185
Day 30: Total Dependence on God		189

Closing Thoughts	193
Notes	195
About the Author	196

Preface

When I first sat down to write the following diary entry, I didn't realize what I was actually admitting to until the words began to flow like a river. It was the first time that I brought to the forefront of my conscious the fact that I was in a vulnerable state of mind. My anticipation for God's promises, coupled with my fleshly strongholds, led me down a road to impatience and deep-seeded pride, both of which I didn't know how to remove by simply thinking it away. This diary entry forced me to face the fact that I needed God more than I understood, and I needed to trust His word more than I ever had—thus came the breakthrough of my *midnight experience*.

Midnight Love

A Diary Entry from August 10, 2016

Midnight is the darkest hour of the night. It's also the scariest and most debilitating. My pupils are dilated the most at that time because I can't seem to find any light for assurance of the path forward. At midnight, I'm anxious and desperate for what feels like a nightmare to be over. Have you ever felt like you can't wake up out of your bad dream? That's me at midnight.

I cry often at midnight. It's mostly out of frustration with my own self because as much as I try (and believe me, I do try), I can't shake off the stagnant pain inside of me. It feels like a heavy weight that rests within my core and refuses to lift up. At midnight, the weight of my world gets even heavier, so much so that it feels unbearable. That's when the walls start closing in.

The emotional pain that finds me at midnight is worse than any physical pain I could ever endure.

No one else knows about my encounters at midnight. I can only describe bits and pieces, but I don't think anyone really gets it. Maybe it's because they can't fathom such a place. Maybe it's because they, too, are dealing with their own darkness and don't have room for engaging in mine.

But after midnight comes and goes—after daybreak hits and my chains from the dark are loosed—I continuously realize that I do love midnight. I even admire it. It calls me to be most attentive to my God—my Lord and Savior. After all, midnight is where He often finds me, emptied of strength, pride, and bravery. It's the time where He pours what's lost back into my soul. He saves me from my own demise.

In my solitude of midnight, God is the One I often find as well. His arms are open wider then, covering me until the morning light shines through. We get through midnight together.

Because I cannot see in the dark, my other senses are heightened. My spiritual senses are awakened. I can hear God's voice. I can feel God's presence. I can taste God's sweet grace and mercy.

I boldly confess that I am both at my weakest and full of untapped strength at midnight. I'm also utterly frightened but feel the safest at midnight. For both truths, it's because I know

Preface

God's caring for me and carrying me through my darkness.

Even though I don't know for certain when I will see the light of daybreak through the dark skies, I know that it will come in due time—in His perfect timing. That divine trust allows me to tell myself, You can get through this, Elana. Yes, even you.

Introduction

Dr. Martin Luther King, Jr. spoke about this subject in his 1964 sermon entitled *A Knock at Midnight*. In the midst of discussing the state of the Christian church, he stated that midnight is the most confusing hour for man where he is wavering on his faith. He also stated that our eternal hope is knowing that midnight only lasts for a moment and that dawn will eventually come. While that idea was over fifty years ago and spoken over a specific event, its sentiment still holds true today: People are desperate for a God-size breakthrough in their situation.

No one specifically asks for midnight to come into their life. No one looks forward to the darkness—the chaos, the confusion, and the distorted perception of reality—that hovers over them like the thickness of night. Most times, people don't even realize they're experiencing midnight until they're already deep within it. By that time, it makes no sense to turn around even though moving toward what lies ahead seems worse. All you can do is ask, "How did I end up here?" and "Why is this happening to *me*?"

People find themselves in a midnight experience for a number of reasons. This book focuses specifically on one: waiting on God's promises to come to pass in your life. In other words, it is the difference between God's timing and yours. It's the realization that God's ways are not your ways in the least bit. Making sense of the fact that there is indeed a difference in how you think versus how God thinks is hard enough to accept, but continuing to wait on Him can sometimes lead us into a cycle of discouragement, doubt, and everything in between. For that reason, your midnight can either be Satan's playground or God's training ground.

Perhaps this is where you are right now. You felt in your heart that God has spoken a promise to you. It encouraged you in the moment because it was exactly what you needed to hear. It was the answer above all answers to your current life situation. It was the type of response that would have been meaningless if it had come from anyone else on this earth. Whether He said it through the avenue of someone else, a sermon, a song, or through a Bible passage, you were confident that it was meant specifically for you. Hearing it gave you inner peace and the strength to continue on your journey with optimism and hope.

You did well for a while holding onto that promise. You maintained encouragement and woke up each morning to the possibilities that God could and would bring you. You even had a little pep in your step, peeking around each corner of your days as if you were waiting for His promise to pop out at you and yell, "Surprise!" But as the days carried on, the pep in your step became a little slower, and your optimism started to diminish — *still no evidence of a promise*. For some of you, those days turned into months. For some of you, like me, those months turned into years.

As time continues, you feel your heart growing weary. It's not necessarily because of any new situation occurring; rather, it's because nothing has really changed, at least not in the way you expected to see and not in the timeframe you expected to see it. You now find yourself in a place where you're questioning everything you once believed:

- *Did I hear God correctly?*

Introduction

- *What should I do to make this blessing actually happen?*
- *Did God forget about me?*
- *Is my faith not strong enough?*

The internal process of questioning not only creates doubt within our spirit, but it also invites mental anguish and the elimination of internal peace. It's not a fun place to be in, and it ultimately causes us to just wish we were out of this season, even if God is simply trying to teach us something along the way. I know about these feelings all too well.

My Story

I considered myself the *everywoman*: I had a good paying job that kept a roof above my head. I had friends and family to turn to when I needed them most. I was well-rounded in my day-to-day lifestyle and felt as though I was blessed to have everything I needed. When people saw me, they were impressed by all the great things I had going on and what I'd accomplished. What they didn't see was the darkness that hovered over me and clouded my internal peace.

You see, years ago, God made two promises to me at different times. Both promises were equally important to me and would change my life trajectory.

The first was an answer to my question about who would be my husband. I prayed often about that question because I didn't want to move forward without God's spiritual blessing and direction, especially since I felt sincere love for the man I was currently dating. When I sensed His confirmation, I was in the middle of a verbal prayer while driving down the highway. God interrupted my words and gave me an impression that I couldn't deny. It wasn't an audible voice, but it was one of the clearest times I ever heard Him speak, so much so that I pulled over to the emergency lane and embraced the peace that overwhelmed me in that moment. While He didn't tell me when a marriage would actually come to pass, He did say it would only happen if I put Him first above all else. That seemed easy enough, right? Gosh, was I wrong. I carried on with my life expecting my circumstance to change just like God said it would. When it didn't, I became discouraged and confused about what I really heard and what He really meant.

The second promise was just as memorable for me eight months later. I was in a season of prayer and fasting. I remember reading my Bible when a particular scripture stood out to me. In fact, it ignited a flame within me. I instantly felt a strong desire to teach biblical principles on a larger scale. God must have known that I needed a little more proof that I heard Him correctly, so a few days later, He gave me a vision of being on a stage teaching women about the Word of God. I knew for certain that God was calling me to something greater than what I was currently doing. He also told me that my calling wouldn't happen immediately. It would take time for Him to groom me so that I could be ready for such a purpose. Little did I know He meant I had to go through some difficult life experiences to learn about the God I was appointed to teach others about.

Both promises kept me excited, but also kept me on edge. Looking back, I don't know if I would've had enough faith for them had I known the amount of stretching they both entailed along the way. For years, I went through bouts of depression and sadness as a result of impatiently waiting on God to move. Along with it, I experienced anxiety, heaviness in my heart, and simply feeling as if I didn't have control over what was happening in my life. It was internal chaos at its finest. The scariest part was that I couldn't shake it off. I mean, I was used to having control over my life, which was how I became successful in my career and other ventures; but not this time. This time was different. I felt like my hands were tied behind my back while I was in a fight for my inner peace. It was awful.

While I was operating as if bad things were happening *to* me, God was trying to show me what miracles He wanted to do *through* me. (Miracles don't come without a period of hardships first, but more on that later.) During that time, I continuously prayed to God that He would remove my negative feelings and restore me back to the comfort of peace and certainty. While I can say now that He was present through it all, I worried back then that He abandoned me at my worst.

I called this journey my midnight experience because it was something so out of the ordinary for me. Prior to that experience, I never had to intentionally trust God for something so grand, and it shook me to do so. The period of time felt like an eternity and it was a struggle to see through the darkness. I was depressed. I was emotional. I was desperate for a conclusion.

However, it was within that season of my life that I discovered a different side of God. I experienced Him as a counselor and a comforter. For the first time ever, I understood what it truly meant to know that He would never leave me or forsake me. That season of waiting drew me closer to Him, and I know it will do the same for you.

You may not be as deep in turmoil as I was, or maybe you are. Regardless, you likely question what to do while you're waiting on God, however long that wait takes. The primary aim of this book is to get you to a place of peace and help you identify what fundamental truths you should be learning along the way. God, in His infinite power, will cover the rest. (I'll uncover more about the key takeaways from the book at the end, but for now, let's start with this general theme.)

A Note about Psalm 119

Psalm 119 is the longest psalm and longest chapter in the entire Bible. It's broken up into the 22 letters of the Hebrew alphabet, thus making it an acrostic poem. Although the author is not known, many scholars believe that it was David, Ezra, or even Daniel. All three men faced difficult seasons in their life (as told in their own books of the Bible) that could accurately be described within the psalm.

The overarching theme of Psalm 119 is that God's word encompasses all we need as believers. If we adore and trust His words, then we are also showing love and honor to the One who spoke them. The two cannot be separated, nor should we want them to be.

To this day, there are several religious figures who recite Psalm 119 as a regular practice. For example, in some Christian sects, monks even recite the psalm as a prayer during the midnight hour. Imagine that.

This poem and prayer is a wonderful teacher of this concept of waiting on God and maintaining peace in the midst of it. The psalmist could have been anyone. He could have been you or me. After all, he, too, was desperate to know God more. He, too, battled with allowing God to handle his conflicts instead of taking matters into his own hands. Even more so, he was holding onto God's promises and waiting to see them come to pass in his life. If there is any text that could relate to you, inspire you, and ultimately lead to your transformation of thought, it's Psalm 119.

How to Navigate this Book

Before you proceed further, you should know about the uniqueness of what you're reading. It's a book and devotional all in one for your convenience and increased focus. Its content is broken into themes that will guide you through your thirty days of intentional devotion.

Let me be clear about something: By no means would I ever guarantee God's promises being fulfilled at the end of your thirty days. That's not my role as a fellow believer and guide. I can, however, assure you that through prayer, intention, and an open heart, you'll be sure to shift your mindset in the following ways:

Current Reality	**Transformed Reality**
I am growing impatient waiting on God.	*I'm increasing my endurance and learning how to be more patient while waiting on God.*
I cannot understand God's ways.	*I accept that I'll never fully understand God, but I trust that His ways will always be better than mine.*

Introduction

Current Reality	Transformed Reality
I don't see any change in my life.	God has a plan and is working things out to prepare me for what He's promised me, even if my natural eyes can't see it.

To get the most out of the book in your hand, I encourage you to adhere to the sections that it is already divided into. At the beginning of each week, take time to read the introductory section. This is intended to frame what you're reading with a central idea and focus. Then, each day contains a different devotion for you to work through with added journal space for reflection and prayer.

At the end of each week, preferably your weekend time, there is a space to go back through your prior five devotions before moving to the following week. (Some of the most profound new messages I receive from the Holy Spirit are when I return to what He's already revealed.) To close out the week, there is more prose that will highlight some points that were made throughout the week. Overall, the book is made to be interactive and an opportunity for reflective meditation.

My encouragement and suggestions through the book come not from a pastoral background or scholarly doctrine per se. Instead, they are from my relatable journey as a child of God and a continuous learner of His ways. I believe what makes us all beautifully human is that we can create a connection with each other through our lived experiences and our lessons learned. The Bible tells us in Revelation 12:11 that we overcome the enemy by the blood of the Lamb and the word of our testimony (NLT). In this book, allow my testimony to speak to you. I pray that God uses what He imparted within me during my midnight experience to encourage you in yours.

Section One

Day One through Day Seven

A Chiropractic Realignment from God

A couple of years ago, I invited a friend to hang out with me at a women's show. This was an annual event held in my city for decades running, and it was usually the highlight of the spring season for Southern ladies alike. From its feminine advertisements and color schemes to flocks of beautiful women all around, the event was a representation of everything I needed in that moment and every moment this time of year: a reminder of who I am as a woman and what I contribute to this world.

This year proved itself to be satisfying, similar to the previous years. As we walked the large auditorium, we saw that there was a wealth of free samples at the booths lined up throughout the building. There were clothes and other useful but unnecessary things to purchase that promised to set you apart from the rest. In the center of the auditorium, there was a runway with the hottest musical artists singing—one after the other—while gorgeous models walked a runway. Everyone eyed them and the newest line of clothing they advertised.

My friend and I enjoyed the walk around the auditorium tasting free treats, touching soft fabrics, and eyeing all the sights. About ninety minutes into our experience, when we felt like we had seen just about everything there was to see, we walked towards the exit to leave. Unexpectedly, an exhibit straight ahead stopped us in our tracks. It caught our attention and our eyes were fixated on a particular demonstration at a booth that we had yet to see. We didn't want to leave without taking a look.

It was rather difficult to see because there was a crowd of people standing around to watch as well. We had to stretch out our necks just a little farther to get a full glimpse of what was occurring. *What is this?* I said to myself, peering at the man speaking and demonstrating. Hearing the crowd's chatter was enough to get us to stand there a little longer, but little did I know that what he offered was what I needed most that day.

Suddenly, the crowd shifted and we were able to get a full view. A chiropractor, wearing a doctor's coat and a cordless microphone, was massaging a woman's back as she sat in a chair leaned forward. As he performed the massage, he explained what he was doing to the woman's spinal cord and why it mattered. While describing his method, the crowd oohed and awed. My friend and I couldn't help to join in, too.

We stood there for three more rounds of demonstrations on different people before I decided to take a turn. Having never been to a chiropractor before, I wanted to see if he was all he was cracked up to be in a five-minute procedure on my own back.

The chiropractor pressed on different parts of my spine and described what each portion impacted – things I didn't even realize mattered to that single spine of mine. Ultimately, it took him only five minutes to convince me that I was in need of a proper realignment if I wanted to experience better health conditions. I made an appointment to get a more thorough exam at his office the very next week.

Had I not gone to the women's show that day with my friend, I wouldn't have had such an encounter that would completely change how I viewed some of my current health problems—ones I surrendered to for so long. In fact, I almost didn't go to the wom-

A Chiropractice Realignment from God

en's show at all. I just didn't feel up to it, but I decided to go in the final hours of the last day it would be there.

I wonder how many of you are in need of an encounter that would completely change the way you perceive your problems—those situations and circumstances that continuously show up in your life and distort your reality. How many of you just simply need a reality check to snap you out of your chaos into focus on what really matters? I have good news for you. There is an ultimate encounter that is readily available for you.

You may have heard about an encounter from God. You may have even had a few, I'm sure. This particular encounter that I'm referring to, though, is one that will completely disrupt your comfort level because it's going to require a little more faith and a lot more stretching. It's the breakthrough that you've been looking for and the peace that you've been praying about. This particular encounter will require a chiropractic-style realignment, the kind that only God can give.

I define *realignment* from God as one that shifts and moves figurative mountains out of your way so that your spirit can focus on the One who really matters. See, anyone can access God, but many people aren't in alignment with Him to do so. As a result, some pray and pray, toil and toil, but still don't feel as if they are hearing God. This leads to even more doubt and anguish rather than the peace they are looking for.

An example of this happened during a conversation I had with a woman at church. We talked for a while about how quickly the year had gone by. (At the time, November was approaching, and we were discussing goals for the New Year.) She proceeded to share that this had been an extremely difficult year for her and she was now trying to hear from God about why she struggled so much this year. Ultimately, she wanted Him to explain her sorrow and current state so she could have more peace and understanding about it.

In that moment, I felt compelled to encourage her with biblical examples of how God speaks to His children, but she cut me off in mid-sentence and moved onto another subject! This happened two more times, and although I was thrown off by it, I attempted to encourage her one last time because she kept coming back to the topic of her frustrations. When I reminded her of the popular verse, *"Be still and know that I am God,"* she told me in a matter-of-fact way that she was indeed sitting still, implying that staying put wasn't her issue as to why she couldn't hear God. Hearing her response, I couldn't help but ask the bigger question that was really on my heart.

"But is your *mind* still, too?" I asked in a softer voice. She paused for a moment. Then she admitted that her mind was always racing and was frequently anxious. Funny how I already knew that was the truth.

The Power of Stillness

If we are going to receive a realignment from God, what we are really saying is that we want Him to move in our life in a mighty way. In order for God to do that, it is up to us to get in position so that He can work. If I hadn't gone to the women's show and even sat in the chiropractor's chair, I know for sure I wouldn't have taken steps to address some deeply rooted health issues in my body. If my church member didn't still her mind and place her focus on God, how could she hear from Him about those answers for which she was seeking Him in the first place?

To still your mind is to quiet your mind. Modern society and culture are both full of noise and our daily lives are filled with chaotic moments. Here are some examples:

- We are burdened about when and how we spend our money
- We stress over the relational connection between ourselves and others
- We dwell on the past and worry ourselves with our future

This list can go on and on. On top of all of that, we Christians work hard to measure up to what we perceive is pleasing to God. If we're not careful, we can find ourselves on a hamster wheel trying to pursue some type of peace and certainty that we'll never grasp. That is why we have to be intentional about quieting our mind and focusing our attention on the One—the only One—who can increase our money and create strong relationships while also healing us from our past.

If you're like I was at one point, you may be struggling with the concept of quieting your mind. As I mentioned earlier, our modern-day culture is built on an unsteady foundation of busyness and anxiousness, so how do we possibly counteract that? Maybe that's why methods to create inner peace are becoming more and more popular, such as mindfulness, yoga, and meditation. People are desperate for a release from that internal pressure system.

What does a Quiet Mind *Sound* Like?

A quiet mind is one with much less talking than normal. At this point, it's common knowledge that people speak tens of thousands of words per day. Obviously, those words would occur in regular conversations, singing to oneself, or even thinking out loud. But imagine making an effort to decrease the number of words and conversations you spoke per day. How much more focused would you be? How much more could you hear God's voice? Speaking less would require becoming more conscious of what you're saying, when you're saying it, and how much you're actually saying about it.

A quiet mind sounds like much less talking to others about your problems. When you are engaging in conversation or a vent session with someone else about something you're displeased with in your life, you may think that you are simply getting heat off your chest. In actuality, what you're really doing is evoking more emotion about it. Not only that, you're reminding yourself of the emotions you already had brewing about it. Think of it like a fire that is trying to burn out, but you continue to add more gas, which ignites it all over again. That's the same thing that you're doing when you continue to engage in conversation about it. Retelling is reigniting, and reigniting only makes that issue your primary focus. God will not reach deep into your thoughts if they are focused on something else.

What does a Quiet Mind *Look* Like?

Simply put, quiet minds appear to others as if you're focused and concentrated. When was the last time you looked at a person and assessed their disposition? As relational people, we do it quite often. Anyone who is intuitive or self-aware will assess someone else's disposition to determine whether or not to engage them in conversation or even how to engage them. For that reason, if you're working on creating a quieter mind, you want people to see it in your disposition. This begins with speaking less, but also leads into expressing less as well.

If someone were to describe you in this season, what would they say? "You look stressed." "You look sad." Here's one that seems to always coerce me into an explanation of my feelings: "You look like something's wrong." While something may indeed be distressing within, or while you may feel bothered in some way, you don't need your disposition to demonstrate it because it only leads you to talk about it. If anything, you'd want someone to say that you appear focused.

Now, God is not expecting you to hold in your thoughts until you combust. There are times when you need to get out your feelings and release some of the tension, and I do understand that. At the same time, you are the captain of your own ship, and it is up to you to determine just how much you share, when you share, and why you're sharing in the first place. God needs you to share it with Him so He can deal with it, because He's the only One who can. The sooner you internalize that truth, the easier it will be for you to filter through your temptation and desires.

What does a Quiet Mind *Feel* Like?

Acquired peace. Much needed rest. Deep inhales and exhales.

A Chiropractice Realignment from God

Those are the phrases that I would use to best describe what a quiet mind feels like. It certainly won't happen immediately. I mean, if it did, then it would be much easier to attain and you wouldn't need a book about it. However, it will indeed happen if you are intentional, speak less, and focus.

When I go to the gym to exercise, I like to play my music to get in the mood. I never go to the gym without my earplugs for that very reason. Often times, I plug in to my favorite songs on my phone on the way to the gym so that I can get a head start on my mood booster. And when I do, I feel my energy increasing. Although it doesn't happen immediately, I can actually feel it coming on more and more.

That is the same way it feels to still your mind, but instead of more energy to move, you experience more energy to be quiet. Essentially, your mind is becoming more relaxed. When you're more relaxed, God has room to enter your mind and heart to speak.

As you can see, the look, sound, and feel of a still and quiet mind are all interconnected. When you speak less about your issues or circumstances, you can become more focused and concentrated. If you are intentionally focused on God and not on your problems, you have the opportunity to feel more peace and rest. Now, you are better able to get in position—or proper alignment—to hear from God.

Getting in position is where the journey of waiting on God's promises begins. Welcome to the other side of your darkness! See, when God places promises on our heart, He is hovering around our circumstances waiting for the right time to bring it to pass. But one thing I had to learn the hard way was that God will not bless what is not in alignment with Him and His word. Therefore, if you're not still and you're not in position, are you *really* ready for what He has in store for you? It's a tough question to ask yourself, but an honest one.

The First Step

There was one other thing that the woman at our local church mentioned to me when she admitted her mind wasn't still. She told me

The Midnight Experience

that she didn't regularly read her Bible and needed to improve on her prayer life. Many Christians don't realize it, but reading your Bible and praying is the way that God speaks to you the most. After all, the Bible is the living word of God. Perhaps you've heard it said before: His words are the same yesterday, today, and forevermore. They are as truthful as they were when He first spoke them. They possess the exact same amount of strength, power, and comfort that they did thousands of years ago. Aren't you glad that you serve a God who is consistent and faithful? Why wouldn't you want to hear His words with His own voice?

Reading the Bible and praying to God is what your first five devotions will be about. The purpose of this is to start from a firm foundation with God. It is the first step to getting into position to hear God's voice.

As you prepare your heart to begin reading the scriptures and the devotions to follow, it is important that you've searched deep down within yourself to assess your salvation. If you can be honest with yourself, you may admit that you've turned away from rightful living. Maybe you previously sought forgiveness for your sins, but know that you've behaved in ways that were not exhibiting God's best for your life. On the other hand, maybe you've never asked God for forgiveness before, but know that you want to have a relationship with Him to seek an inner peace that the world could never give you. With either circumstance, now is a good time to stop what you're doing and pray a prayer of forgiveness for your sins. Romans 10:9-10 then tells us that if *"we confess with our mouth and believe with our heart that God raised Jesus from the dead, we will be saved"* (NLT). If you are ready to have a fresh start in your walk with God, You can repeat the following prayer:

> *Dear Heavenly Father, I thank You for sending Your son to save me from myself. I ask You, Father, to forgive me of all my sins, to cleanse me, and to make me new. I believe that You can give me the strength to live for You all the days of my life. I ask these things in Jesus' name, amen.*

A Chiropractice Realignment from God

If you prayed that prayer, then you have received a new beginning through Jesus Christ. Not only that, you've walked the first steps of getting into position to hear from God, your Father with the confidence that He is with you.

Now, the hardest part of your spiritual walk is not saying the prayer above; rather, it's living it out on a daily basis for the rest of your life, especially when you've been accustomed to living differently than what God requires. In fact, many of the stories in the Bible shed light on how difficult it is for God's children to stay on the right path. That's why He gives us grace for the tough times.

As you read Psalm 119, you'll see how the psalmist struggles with his own right-minded living, too. It seemed as if he was intentionally telling himself of who God was to him. It's no coincidence that the beginning of Psalm 119 is introducing us to what the psalmist cares about most and what He's focused on. It also teaches us that he, too, is getting himself in position to get a chiropractic realignment done. Hopefully, you'll understand from his own prayers that in this walk with God, the journey is much more important than the destination.

So quiet your mind, open your heart, and be ready for an encounter with the One who's been waiting on your surrender. He's not looking for perfection. He's looking for *you*—all of you. Let's move to your weekly devotions.

Day 1

Who are the Happiest Ones of All?

Today I will

- recognize the importance of following all of God's word as the start of my transformation.

- perform an inspection of my heart, searching for areas that need to be cleaned out.

Aleph

¹ Joyful are people of integrity,
who follow the instructions of the LORD.
² Joyful are those who obey his laws
and search for him with all their hearts.
³ They do not compromise with evil,
and they walk only in his paths.
⁴ You have charged us
to keep your commandments carefully.
⁵ Oh, that my actions would consistently
reflect your decrees!
⁶ Then I will not be ashamed
when I compare my life with your commands.
⁷ As I learn your righteous regulations,
I will thank you by living as I should!
⁸ I will obey your decrees.
Please don't give up on me!

Psalm 119:1-8 NLT

Let's Talk about It

Law. That word sounds so strict. With every generation, there has been a movement of rebellion against the strict laws that *restrict* one's ability to simply be. Maybe that's why some have a hard time following God's laws.

In the biblical days, it was also difficult for God's chosen people to follow what He required of them. Sometimes I feel as if I'm right there with them—making choices that are so opposite of what God wants. It's a good thing that we have a God who is merciful and a Savior who already paid the price for our sins so that even when we do fall, we're given the grace to move on guilt-free and punishment-free.

All of God's laws, precepts, and commandments were not meant to restrict us from being; rather, they were meant to set us apart from the rest of the world to raise the standard for the way we lived and loved. The sooner we know and believe that, the easier it will be to walk in His ways. After all, God promises that abundant blessings will flow from our belief and obedience.

It took me years to fully understand this concept. I spent my time focusing on what felt good to my flesh rather than living from God's best. Because of that, I couldn't *receive* God's best. Think of it like this: God won't bless our deliberate sins. He just won't.

The first step to moving from your midnight to your daybreak is to intentionally pursue a better way to live. This doesn't mean that we're expected to get it right every time, because the Lord knows we won't. It does mean, though, that we will be honest, focused, and humble through our pursuit of rightful living.

Day 1 Devotional

Digging Deeper

Before you can proceed, it is critical that you ask God to search your heart. What is it that you've held onto for so long and haven't released? Pride? Greed? Doubt? Guilt?

_____

_____

_____

_____

_____

Ask God for forgiveness for whatever area is holding you down, and then ask God to give you the strength to release it. Remember: This release is not a temporary fix only to relapse the next time you are weak. You have to fully let it go so that you can begin to build your life on a foundation of God's righteousness.

Prayer

God, thank You for your continuous mercy and patience. I pray that You search my heart and reveal to me those things that are keeping me from operating with pureness. Show them to me, Lord, so that I may seek Your forgiveness of them and release them. Help me to obey You with full submission and pursuit. Amen.

Day 2

The Rhythm of God

Today I will

- identify ways to stay committed to my pursuit of God.

Beth

⁹ *How can a young person stay pure?*
By obeying your word.
¹⁰ *I have tried hard to find you—*
don't let me wander from your commands.
¹¹ *I have hidden your word in my heart,*
that I might not sin against you.
¹² *I praise you, O LORD;*
teach me your decrees.
¹³ *I have recited aloud*
all the regulations you have given us.
¹⁴ *I have rejoiced in your laws*
as much as in riches.
¹⁵ *I will study your commandments*
and reflect on your ways.
¹⁶ *I will delight in your decrees*
and not forget your word.

Psalm 119:9-16 NLT

Let's Talk about It

Yesterday was about obtaining rightful living. Today is about maintaining it. Many times, it's much easier to gain something than it is to maintain it. There must be a system, routine, or even a rhythm in place to keep what you have; otherwise, you will find yourself back at square one, as if you never even obtained it.

Pursuing God is no different. When I first began to hear God's voice and feel His presence, I was on a natural high, to say the least. I felt like I had reached a level of peace that I hadn't before. But not long after, life happened. Busyness happened. Distractions happened. Before I knew it, I was out of sync, or rhythm, with God's way of living.

The rhythm. It's what we all need in order to maintain our relationship with God and to follow His ways. Without it, we are bouncing back and forth between our "usual life" and our pursuit of a better one.

The psalmist is transparent about trying to stay pure and on the right side of living. He realized that his best option was to obey God's every word and to hide it in his heart. He teaches us to do the same.

God's word is His love story to you; therefore, God the being and God's word cannot be separated; to honor One is to honor the other. And there are many ways to honor Him, such as reading His word and praying. If you can commit to doing these at least once per day, you will find the two-step that will keep you in sync with God's.

Day 2 Devotional

Digging Deeper

It's all about the rhythm with God. Without a clear rhythm, you are just dancing around, *hoping* to stay on beat with Him. In what ways can you maintain your daily rhythm as you journey with God? List them out here.

_____

_____

_____

_____

Now take a step further by breaking down each item you listed. When and what time will you complete them? How long? Get as specific as possible to ensure you're committing to a new habit.

_____

_____

_____

_____

Prayer

God, thank you for Your patience as I learn to seek You more. You know that my desire is there, but my flesh wants to go back to the "old ways." Help me to remain disciplined in my pursuit. Plant Yourself in my heart as I draw closer. I'm determined to be in rhythm with You. Beat the drum so I can follow. Amen.

Day 3

Set Me Apart

Today I will

- recognize what it means to really be a servant of God.

Gimel

¹⁷ Be good to your servant,
that I may live and obey your word.
¹⁸ Open my eyes to see
the wonderful truths in your instructions.
¹⁹ I am only a foreigner in the land.
Don't hide your commands from me!
²⁰ I am always overwhelmed
with a desire for your regulations.
²¹ You rebuke the arrogant;
those who wander from your commands are cursed.
²² Don't let them scorn and insult me,
for I have obeyed your laws.
²³ Even princes sit and speak against me,
but I will meditate on your decrees.
²⁴ Your laws please me;
they give me wise advice.

Psalm 119:17-24 NLT

Let's Talk about It

What does it mean to be God's servant? When we think of the term, it can be described in simplest terms as our obedience to God and our allegiance to Him. This makes total sense; after all, Psalm 119 is about God's word, and one of Christians' primary struggles is our ultimate obedience to it. Time and again we fall short, similar to the way we try to break bad habits and form new ones.

When we commit to God and His word, we discover a new, more alive way of living and being. Contrary to the misguided mind, there is freedom in following His word—more freedom than the world could ever give. It's no wonder that the psalmist prays for his eyes to be open; with God, you will see a completely different view. That's what it means to be set apart.

Jeremiah 33:3 says it best: *"Call to me, and I'll answer you. I'll tell you beautiful and wondrous things you could never figure out on your own"* (The Message).

When we pursue Him by being committed to His word, He promises to reveal things to us that we've never seen before. Who wouldn't want more of that?

Notice that in 119:21, the tone switches rather abruptly to how the psalmist is being treated by others. Don't be alarmed—this occurs pretty often. As we draw closer to God, the enemy tries even harder to attack us. It's his way of separating us from God because He knows God will never separate Himself from us. Unexpectedly, it can sometimes occur through the slander and criticism of other people.

Have you ever felt like the better you start to feel on the inside, the worse others try to make you feel all around you? It's definitely not a coincidence. It's best to take the psalmist's advice here to continue to meditate on God's word. He will give you the counsel of how to deal with others so that you can continue to focus on Him.

Day 3 Devotional

Digging Deeper

Let's make the idea of being God's servant much more personal. What does it mean in your life to be His servant? What could it look like, sound like, and feel like? Write those down below.

_____

_____

_____

How have you experienced the enemy trying to attack you? Maybe it's through the words of others. The psalmist prayed about how He wanted God to handle his enemies. It's important that we model this. Write a prayer and be specific about how you want God to deal with your enemies. I recommend praying this prayer whenever you feel the attacks coming on. It is another way to help you remain focused on God, not distracted by others.

_____

_____

_____

Prayer

God, I now see myself as Your servant and I'm no longer alone. You're a part of me as I draw closer to You. I pray that You continue to show me what I haven't seen and take me where I've never been as I work to follow You. Block the enemy's tactics to take away my focus. Set me apart from my enemies, just as I see myself. Amen.

Day 4

The Pressure is On

Today I will

- recognize that God is greater than any pressure that comes my way.

- identify the real issues that are hidden beneath my surface.

Daleth

^{25} I lie in the dust;
revive me by your word.
^{26} I told you my plans, and you answered.
Now teach me your decrees.
^{27} Help me understand the meaning of your commandments,
and I will meditate on your wonderful deeds.
^{28} I weep with sorrow;
encourage me by your word.
^{29} Keep me from lying to myself;
give me the privilege of knowing your instructions.
^{30} I have chosen to be faithful;
I have determined to live by your regulations.
^{31} I cling to your laws.
Lord, don't let me be put to shame!
^{32} I will pursue your commands,
for you expand my understanding.

Psalm 119:25-32 NLT

Let's Talk about It

Lord, things are getting heavy now. It's becoming harder to focus on You with all that is happening around me. I'm sad. I'm burdened. I'm stressed. Help!

There have been too many times to count how often I've prayed those words out loud. I believe this is where believers begin to lose their faith and hope—when the pressure is on to trust God during the most uncomfortable times. The more we grow in our closeness to God and our understanding of His language, the more we are given to bear, withstand, and be responsible for what comes our way. This includes what we are given emotionally, too. It's not a punishment; it's a promotion of responsibility. Frankly, it's a pleasure-pain experience.

But wait: What happens when the darkness that we've tried so hard to bury resurfaces? What do we do when our frustrations are tackling us with full force?

First and foremost, we must pray about it. During that prayer, we must admit our issues and concerns to God just as the psalmist did. I'm not talking about the surface-level prayers that share "just enough" to get the point across. I'm referring to the prayers that hurt to even say out loud. The ones that confess your real issues or concerns beneath the surface.

You may be saying to yourself, "But I've never shared those things with anyone before!" Good. Those are the ones God is waiting to hear from you.

Take another look at verse 29. Sometimes the biggest lies we hear are the ones we tell our own self, which is all the more reason we need God's wisdom to be able to filter through them. (I don't know about you, but there have been plenty of times I didn't even realize I was lying to myself!) What are those ideas or thoughts that are keeping you awake at night? Trade those in for obedience and trust in God's truths.

Day 4 Devotional

Digging Deeper

It's time to get honest with yourself and your God. What things are *really* bothering you? What's *really* keeping you unfocused and awake at night?

_____

_____

_____

_____

Now, let's take it a step further: What lies have you been telling yourself for so long? Remember: God can't bless your lies. He needs you to recognize them so that He can transform them.

_____

_____

_____

Prayer

God, thank You for Your wisdom and continued pursuit of me. I have some things to share with You that I don't typically say out loud. I'm ready to be honest with myself so that You can begin to heal my broken places and fill them with Your everlasting truths. Give me grace, God. This has been a long time coming. Amen.

Day 5

The True Source of Happiness

Today I will

- understand the importance of prayer to seek understanding of God's word.

- recognize that nothing can replace knowing God and being loved by Him.

He

> [33] *Teach me your decrees, O LORD;*
> *I will keep them to the end.*
> [34] *Give me understanding and I will obey your instructions;*
> *I will put them into practice with all my heart.*
> [35] *Make me walk along the path of your commands,*
> *for that is where my happiness is found.*
> [36] *Give me an eagerness for your laws*
> *rather than a love for money!*
> [37] *Turn my eyes from worthless things,*
> *and give me life through your word.*
> [38] *Reassure me of your promise,*
> *made to those who fear you.*
> [39] *Help me abandon my shameful ways;*
> *for your regulations are good.*
> [40] *I long to obey your commandments!*
> *Renew my life with your goodness.*

Psalm 119:33-40 NLT

The Midnight Experience

Let's Talk about It

I spent many years trying to compensate for what was missing in my life. At one point, shopping covered up the emptiness I felt on the inside. Little did I know that the temporary comfort could turn into a full-blown addiction. To add to that, sleep aids were my source of pleasure for fifteen years. I used them to escape the tough times I faced. To add gasoline to the flames, it wasn't until recently that I realized just how much I relied on male companionship for comfort and security.

Despite my best efforts, none of those things were fulfilling although I kept reaching for them as if they were. I had to learn through much internal fighting that nothing—and I do mean nothing—can replace God's love. When we are missing that unique relationship with God, we are left with a void, one that only He can fill.

That void is mended as we continue to pursue God. The psalmist has already given us examples of this:

- Confessing your sins and your desire for a relationship with God
- Creating a routine for maintaining right-minded living
- Following the instructions that God gives
- Recognizing God's greatness over your life and struggles

Here's one more: As you draw closer to God, be sure to pray for clarity of His word. You can't have an authentic relationship if you don't understand each other, right? In doing so, God will make His words clear to you. Not only will it give you peace, but it will also change your mindset. For me, I no longer desired those things that were a temporary fix because I found something (and Someone) greater.

Day 5 Devotional

Digging Deeper

As we draw closer to God and continue to seek understanding, He helps us to understand ourselves in the process. That's how I discovered all those things that I used to fill a void in my life.

Search your heart. Are there things or people that you are using to fill a void in your life? How are they currently filling that void? Write them down as an act of admission and surrender. Then pray for God to remove them.

_____

_____

_____

_____

_____

_____

Prayer

God, I continue to know You in a more personal way. I don't want to just follow You, I want to know You. Please change my old ways of thinking. I no longer want to chase after things that don't matter. Give me clarity and show me a new way of being. I'm determined to pursue You, and I won't stop until I find You. Amen.

Day 6 and 7
Recap and Reflection

Psalm 119:1-40

Go back through this week's reading. Write down any new thoughts that come to mind to deepen your perspective and reflection that you've gained.

_____
_____
_____
_____

Digging Deeper

Is there something you need to dig deeper on this weekend? Explore the things you wrote down this week and see if more revelations come to mind.

_____
_____
_____
_____

Prayer

After going back through this week's readings, write a personal prayer to God. Thank Him for what He's done for you and confess to Him what you've been holding onto this week. Release it into His hands through your prayer.

_____

_____

_____

_____

_____

_____

Endless Supplier

I remember when I first heard about it. I was in my bedroom folding clothes and putting them away in their proper places. I had the television playing in the background so that I could still hear it even though I wasn't directly watching it. I turned to a popular Christian network and was listening to world renowned Pastor Jimmy Evans preach about the topic of marriage. Right smack in the middle of my sock-folding, I heard him say something that made me stop and look directly at the television.

He described how all human beings have four deep needs that can only be met by God: Acceptance, identity, security, and purpose. With each word that he called out, I felt an explosion go through my veins. I knew in that moment that God was trying to get my attention.

Let me back up a bit. Before folding clothes that day, I was experiencing yet another round of deep sadness. My days seemed long and my nights were restless. My job responsibilities were becoming more stressful and less inspiring. I wasn't enjoying it anymore and felt like I was spending more time pushing away frustrations rather than receiving satisfaction. Also, my romantic life was in shambles because my relationship recently ended and I was still mourning the loss of what I thought was a good thing. (What made it worse was that this seemed completely opposite of the promise that I thought God spoke to me about marriage. I was so confused!) Even more so, I wasn't really connecting with my friends anymore and felt as if we just weren't compatible like we used to be.

I felt like my world was in a complete disarray and I had no control of how to rationalize it or even make it better. When I tried to make sense of it, my words turned into complaints. *Lord, where are the promises that You spoke to me?* That was a question I prayed often, desperate to hear something encouraging to hold onto. But God, in His supernatural way, didn't remove my frustrations; instead, He revealed to me the root of them so that I could remove them myself.

One thing that a midnight experience teaches you is how to fully rely on God despite what is occurring (or not occurring) in your life. Understanding the four deepest needs that God created within us helps us to do just that. So let's break them down.

The Deep Need for Acceptance

When we seek approval from others in any capacity, we are experiencing the need to feel accepted and loved. In a work setting, this could occur when we seek praise or acknowledgment from our boss on a project, on words that we speak, or on simply being a "good enough" employee. Many people also attach themselves to organizations or groups—whether that be gangs, Greek sororities and fraternities, church groups, or anything in between—because they want to be a part of a collective. Again, we are naturally inclined to seek belonging.

The Deep Need for Identity

The need for identity usually shows up when we're trying to give ourselves a name or title. Oftentimes, the following questions are behind this need:

What is your identity?
Why is that your identity?
Who gave you that identity?

Similar to the need for acceptance, identity can occur in situations where we are seeking assurance of who we are. In relationships, I often made a big deal about my title and how someone referred to me. For example, I spent a long time arguing with a guy I was romantically involved with about why he should give me the title of girlfriend or wife. I never did so well with simply *being*. In my eyes, that title gave me an identity. It gave me the assurance that I mattered to him. I found this same way of thinking to be true at my job as well. Regardless of what role I was playing and how people treated me, that prestigious title determined how I viewed my own worth. The title that I can throw around at others gave me a power that I didn't think I had by just being Elana Cole.

The Deep Need for Security

The need for security is probably one of the most obvious examples in our life. It becomes very apparent in what we have, who we have, and how much of it we have.

Money is a major security measure in today's culture. We are led to believe that the more wealth we obtain, the less we have to worry and the fewer problems we'll have to deal with. Additionally, job security is always a topic of conversation. To speak on relationships again, having someone alongside us often gives us assurance that we're not alone. Think about it: How many people do you know are afraid to be alone? That was certainly my crutch for a long time.

The Deep Need for Purpose

There's no way of getting around this one: Humankind is in search of significance. Just as with all of the above deep needs, we were created to have a purpose. You've heard stories of people leaving their careers to do something they really love. Those individuals are seeking after their purpose. Even many of those who don't know God are in search of something bigger than themselves. They want to make a difference regardless of whether that is in a grand way or in the simplest ways. To put it plainly, we need more than what the daily grind has to offer.

With each of the deepest needs above, there is an inherent desire that we can't shake off. God created us that way on purpose. When you really think about it, you see that people spend their entire lives searching for their deepest needs in the worldliest of places, only to end up on that same hamster wheel, but in a new cage. What I'm trying to say is that only God can give you those needs. Jesus understood that. The psalmist understood that. Now it's time for you to do the same.

There are plenty of stories in the Bible that reiterate this point, but there is one in particular that really woke me up to this understanding. It's the story of God providing *manna* for His chosen people.

When the Israelites left Egypt, God's main goal was to teach them to rely solely on Him, which is the absolute opposite of how they lived for the past four hundred years. One of the ways He did this was with what He fed them. God ensured that manna, a substance they had never seen before, fell from the sky each day. As He instructed them, the Israelites were only to gather up enough manna for that day to feed themselves and their family. He warned them that if they tried to save any for the next day, it would spoil; however, on Friday, they were to gather enough for the weekend because on Saturday (Jewish Sabbath day), they would rest from gathering manna.

Just like us, the Israelites took a while to fully trust God, even though He promised them He would continuously supply their need to eat. They were used to living in a way that kept what belonged to them because there was no guarantee that they would have it again, especially from the one who led them. So they did the

Endless Supplier

opposite of what God instructed: They gathered and tried to keep some for the next day, but it did indeed spoil, just like He said it would. They tried to go out and gather on the Sabbath, and there was none. But God, in His loving discipline, allowed them to go through this experience to learn just how faithful and trustworthy He is. Eventually, they saw that their former ways of living were no longer needed. If God can demonstrate that to them, what more can He show you if you simply trust Him?

God is an endless supplier of all our needs, especially the deepest ones. The first forty verses of Psalm 119 teach us by the way that the psalmist engages in God and pursues Him. The more he submitted to God's instructions, the more he desired God, and he desired God because God provided for him.

I believe that during this time of waiting on God's promises, He is taking you on a journey to learn how to rely on Him for all your deepest needs. Need more proof? Take a look at the following scriptures:

- **Acceptance:** God loves you and accepts you regardless of how many times you fail (Romans 5:8-11)

- **Identity:** God has made you an heir to the throne (Romans 8:17)

- **Security:** God will never leave you or forsake you (Deuteronomy 31:6)

- **Purpose:** God wants you to glorify His name (Isaiah 43:7)

The beauty of it all is that God is not a "one and done" God. Endless supply means exactly that. When Jesus taught His disciples how to pray, one of the things He said was, *"Give us this day our daily bread"* (Matthew 6:11, NKJV). That daily bread is the provision of God. You can ask Him to fill your needs regularly and He'll provide it, large or small. So go ahead, ask God for what you need and continue to seek His presence while doing it.

Section Two

Day Eight through Day Fourteen

His Demonstration of *True* Love

I recently went to a friend's house to hang out for a few hours. When I arrived, her two daughters, ages five and seven, excitedly greeted me at the door with a big hug. It was mid-afternoon, which was usually their nap time (otherwise known as mommy's cool-down time), but since they apparently weren't doing either of those, I asked them what they were doing instead.

"We're watching a movie! Come look!" they exclaimed. Before I knew it, I was being dragged by the arm to the girls' playroom where there was a new Disney movie playing on the television. Within seconds, the girls proceeded to tell me how much they loved this movie because they thought the princess was so pretty. Not only that, they felt it necessary that I know the plot of how the princess finds a prince charming-type character in the end and they live happily ever after. *Gee, love stories sure haven't changed much since I was a little girl,* I thought to myself.

After I left my "training" on the school of love, I reconnected with my friend. She thought it was hilarious that her daughters were so into the movie and really believed that this was what true love looked like.

"Remember when we were that innocent?" she asked me as we reminisced about our own childhood experiences with animated love story plots.

"Naïve is more like it!" I responded with a headshake and a whole-hearted laugh. I was mostly kidding with that statement, but in a way, I was very serious.

As little girls, we are cultivated to believe that love—true love—can be manufactured into a ninety-minute movie and produce everlasting results. Many little girls spend much of their play time dreaming up how to recreate what they see in the media. I can remember all the times I "played house" and created impressive storylines for my dolls to experience what my young mind perceived as love. Ultimately, the desire for love is deep within us and it doesn't go away.

The young girl philosophy on love usually evolves into the grown woman philosophy of love, and the media does a pretty cunning job of reinforcing this idea to our adult minds just as much as the animated movies did to first cultivate it.

Think about what we're surrounded with. You can't even walk past the magazine aisle of the grocery store without seeing an evaluation of true love: Either celebrity couples are perceived as being incredibly happy or incredibly miserable. Ideally, it's either true love or it's not, and if it's not, there is another shot at true love right around the corner to do this dance all over again.

Television shows and movies are just as bad as the tabloids. Similarly, they portray relationships as either absolutes or replaceable. It seems as if it's only real love in the moment, but after time passes and the relationships become uneventful, people often leave and look for the next best thing. Not only that, when did we reach a point in society where we believed that a person could find his or her soulmate during a competition of thirty other people in twelve episodes? I often wonder if we're just chasing a feeling rather than appreciating the journey.

Honestly, I don't blame the media for its portrayal of love. I mean, while it is indeed skewed, it only proves what I said earlier:

His Demonstration of *True* Love

There is a strong desire within each of us as human beings to know and feel love. Unfortunately, the way we go about it sets us up for misconceptions that God has to come in and correct.

- Common Misconceptions about True Love
- True love just happens and you don't have to work hard to maintain it.
- Strong relationships feel fantastic most of the time.
- Love originated with mankind.
- The perfect person is out there for you and will meet all your needs.
- Love must always be a 50/50 partnership to work.
- Love is supposed to look the way it is depicted in the media.

Now, I could spend time debunking all of these misconceptions for you, but we'll save that for another book. I will, however, emphasize one point that is imperative for you to grasp over anything else: Love did not originate with humankind. It originated with God, and because He loved us first, we now can use that model to demonstrate love back to Him and to others.

See, God's original plan was to make mankind in His image. Out of all the things that God created, we were the only ones that He made to reflect His own likeness. That's how much He cared about us. Not only that, mankind was the only creation that He breathed His breath into so that we could have life connected to Him—His spirit to ours.

> *"Then God said, 'Let us make mankind in our image, in our likeness, so that they may rule over the fish in the sea and the birds in the sky, over the livestock and all the wild animals, and over all the creatures that move along the ground'" (Genesis 1:26 NIV).*

> *"Then the LORD God formed the man from the dust of the*

> *ground. He breathed the breath of life into the man's nostrils, and the man became a living person"* (Genesis 2:7 NLT).

The one thing I love most about the Bible is that it is one big love story. All throughout it, God is demonstrating His love through promises He spoke, grace He gave, and blessings that He distributed to His people. Often times in the Bible, God demonstrates His love to those who messed up enough times that you would think they didn't even deserve it. Well, you're right to think that, because most times, we *are* undeserving of just how much He loves us. But that's what makes God's love immeasurably good. He continues to pursue us, protect us, and love us even when we least deserve it.

In the next five devotions, the psalmist begins to really understand God's love. As you read, you'll notice that he shifts in tone as he grows in his love and reverence for God. In the devotions you've already read, the psalmist has an adornment for His word and His promises. We could infer that he is still seeking to understand what it means to follow God's ways and trust Him completely. Now, you'll see the psalmist emphasize his love for God even more, especially as he watches God transform his broken heart and his tough moments into places of peace. From there, his language is different. His worship increases, too. This is exactly what happens when we are blessed with experiencing just a drop of God's love in our lives.

It's no wonder that the psalmist continues to meditate on God's word regularly throughout this time. He understands the standard that God is setting for him as he draws closer to the only One he can place his hope and faith in. If we're going to be set apart to live a life full of promises that God has gifted to us, we can't live the same way we used to with the same mindsets, complaints, brokenness, or impure thinking. It's like oil and water—they simply don't mix.

In our own lives, as we increase our faith and our commitment to living according to God's standards, we are actually showing our love back to Him. The more committed we are to living for God, the more inclined we are to follow in His ways and see His blessings come to pass in our life. The following two scriptures emphasize that.

His Demonstration of *True* Love

"If you love me, obey my commandments." (John 14:15 NLT).
"Love means doing what God has commanded us, and
he has commanded us to love one another, just as you
heard from the beginning" (2 John 1:6 NLT).

When we come to understand the way God loves and the ways He wants us to demonstrate love back to Him, our love for Him greatly increases. This is the true love that we are all longing for. It's the very thing that leads the psalmist to say in 119:62 that he rises *"at midnight to give thanks to God for the standards He's setting through His regulations"* (NLT). Like the psalmist, the midnight experience will lead us to a heart of gratitude for God's ways as well.

A few years ago, at the beginning stages of my midnight experience, I was taking classes at church for post-divorce recovery. My divorce was finalized six months earlier and I had spent most of that time avoiding the pain of feeling the death of a marriage. It took some time, but I finally admitted to myself that I needed to deal with my emotions that were permeating every area of my life and preventing me from moving forward. I found out about these particular classes and each week, I looked forward to what God could and would do throughout my journey of healing.

Around the third week, I remember walking to the restroom for our mid-class break. I went to grab the paper towel on the counter and randomly looked up at the mirror. For the first time in the three weeks of attending and walking to this same restroom, I decided to read an 8x5 paper taped to the mirror. I saw it there in the previous weeks but never took the time to read the words. It didn't stand out with fancy colors or images, but the words—God's words—finally caught my attention.

"Fear not, for I have redeemed you; I have called you by
your name; You are Mine" (Isaiah 43:1 NKJV).

I stared at the words for a few moments. I felt like God was speaking right to me! I even felt a peace come over me that I hadn't felt in really a long time. The more I stared at the scripture, the more I was convinced God was assuring me that He would take care of me through my entire midnight experience and see me to the other side, simply because He loved me and I belonged to Him. To this day, Isaiah 43:1 is my favorite scripture for that very reason.

I never forgot the feeling I felt when I first saw the scripture on the mirror. It was in a season of feeling low and alone. During a time when many people turn to other avenues for love, such as jumping into another relationship (and believe me when I say I wanted to do just that), God was giving me a gentle reminder that a relationship with Him was actually what I needed most. A personal relationship with Him would be the cure for the internal chaos I possessed. Everything else would flow from it. As my relationship with God increased throughout my midnight experience, He showed me areas of my life that were trapped in bondage. Then, in His perfect love and grace, He worked to free me from them.

Our Bondage + His Love = Healing

Bondage is defined as the state of being a slave or enslaved to something that is controlling you[2]. It can ultimately appear in many forms depending on what is holding us down. On the topic of love, residue from a broken heart and unmet expectations can lead us to a place of crying out to God, wondering where our happy ending is. Unanswered questions about how a former relationship ended can also create an unsettling feeling that we carry around and transfer to others. If not properly tended to, that bondage only becomes tighter around us and leaves us in a captivity that we were never meant to be in. Some people refer to all of this as excess baggage.

I heard a story once about a woman who had an issue with baggage while traveling. She was only going on a three-day trip for work-related purposes, but all of her bags seemed as if she was staying for an entire week. When she approached the counter to check in to her flight, the person at the counter asked her how many bags she was checking in. When she replied by saying she was checking in two bags, plus her two carry-on bags, the clerk looked confused.

Maybe she doesn't realize there is a cost for each bag she checks in, he thought to himself. He proceeded to explain the costs that came along with checking in bags and suggested that she downsize so to only check in one bag instead of two. The woman agreed and moved all of her items from the smaller bag into the larger one. It was tight, but she managed to get everything to fit.

Feeling confident that she would reduce cost, she placed her larger, fuller luggage on the scale to be weighed and checked in. When the clerk saw the number on the scale, he was hesitant to look back at the woman for fear that she would see the judgment he had on his face for such a ridiculous situation.

"Ma'am, unfortunately, your bag now exceeds the weight limit allowed and you will have to incur more costs if you choose to proceed."

Looking visibly frustrated and defeated, the woman realized that time was lapsing and she had no other choice but to incur the additional costs this time. For her, it was a lesson learned that too much baggage leads to hidden costs.

God wants to send you the same lesson. The baggage that you've been carrying around from past experiences is weighing you down. It's also preventing you from moving forward with completeness and ultimate peace. Even if you try to stuff those thoughts, feelings, and memories deep down hoping they'll disappear, I have news for you: They won't. There is always a cost to the excess weight you carry around.

Only God knows how deep your hurt goes. Only God knows what you've been carrying around, despite how well you've been able to disguise it. Let me reiterate that your past hurts don't just go away because time has lapsed. They actually resurface in the most unsuspecting ways, such as in bouts of anger towards someone else who had nothing to do with your prior anger, or like the insecurity that you continue to feel when you approach a new situation. The only way to remove what is weighing you down is to allow God's love to heal you from the inside out.

The Midnight Experience

Regardless of where you are in your relationship with God, your midnight experience is needed so that He can dig up the roots and give you a fresh start. It's not only needed, it is a part of God's perfect plan to show you what true love really looks like. It's meant to slow you down and bring your attention to what God wants you to see rather than what the world does.

Although His love is always available to us, we sometimes hold our own selves back from experiencing it to the fullest because we are caught up in what the world defines as love. This leads to internal thoughts of not being enough or even that we've done too much for Him to love us the way we want. But God's love is unconditional. The sooner we realize that, the more at peace we'll be.

As you move through the devotions this week, take time to also reflect on how God has and is demonstrating His love to you. Take note of what evidence you see around you. Read more scriptures that speak to your heart about His love. This, too, is considered a way to meditate on God's word as the psalmist describes.

Before we move into the devotions, read through more of Isaiah 43. It's definitely a depiction of how and why God loves.

But now, thus says the Lord, who created you, O Jacob, And He who formed you, O Israel:
¹"Fear not, for I have redeemed you; I have called you by your name; You are Mine. ² When you pass through the waters, I will be with you; And through the rivers, they shall not overflow you. When you walk through the fire, you shall not be burned, nor shall the flame scorch you. ³For I am the Lord your God, The Holy One of Israel, your Savior, I gave Egypt for your ransom, Ethiopia and Seba in your place. ⁴Since you were precious in My sight, You have been honored, and I have loved you; therefore I will give men for you, and people for your life. ⁵Fear not, for I am with you; I will bring your descendants from the east, and gather you from the west; ⁶I will say to the north, 'Give them up!' And to the south, 'Do not keep them back!' Bring My sons from afar, and My daughters from the ends of the earth— ⁷Everyone who is called by My name, whom I have created for My glory; I have formed him, yes, I have made him"
(Isaiah 43:1-7 NKJV).

Day 8

Anchored in His Love

Today I will

- identify all the ways God has provided for me.

Waw

*[41] LORD, give me your unfailing love,
the salvation that you promised me.
[42] Then I can answer those who taunt me,
for I trust in your word.
[43] Do not snatch your word of truth from me,
for your regulations are my only hope.
[44] I will keep on obeying your instructions
forever and ever.
[45] I will walk in freedom,
for I have devoted myself to your commandments.
[46] I will speak to kings about your laws,
and I will not be ashamed.
[47] How I delight in your commands!
How I love them!
[48] I honor and love your commands.
I meditate on your decrees.*

Psalm 119:41-48 NLT

Let's Talk about It

Though our midnight is a dark and often frightful place, there is a reason we remain comforted: It's the certainty in knowing that He's there with us. God's presence is felt through the thickness of our emotions. His presence pushes past our fears and pain to refocus our attention on what matters more than any problem we face: His unfailing love.

When we open our Bible, we are expecting God to speak to our hearts about our situation. We are hoping that His answers will give us the confidence to respond to the world and to the people in it who try to keep us from being our best self. As the psalmist declares, God's words are our only hope, and His love is our only peace.

But it's not enough for us to wait for an answer from God. We must remain steady in obeying what He has already commanded us to do. We cannot pick and choose what we want to follow just like we wouldn't want God to pick and choose when He wants to love us.

We each are saved by God's grace, and that unfathomable grace is how He loves us. Even in our darkest hour, and even in our uncertainty, we must willingly follow all God asks of us. Our obedience keeps us anchored in His love because it changes what we see (our perception) and what we seek after (our pursuit). As 1John 5:3 says, we show our love to God by walking in His ways (NLT).

Do you want to know how you, like the psalmist, can walk in freedom? It's through your devotion to what your Lord and Savior asks of you.

Day 8 Devotional

Digging Deeper

Our obedience to God comes when we are faithful to Him in the moment, not just for a future date. Take some time to think on this: What is God asking you to do right now? Maybe it's removing yourself from the company of certain people. Maybe He wants you to stop watching TV or listening to music that promotes the opposite of the life you're aiming to live. Whatever it is, be honest with yourself. Then, begin today by walking in obedience. As a result, you'll discover God's love.

_____

_____

_____

_____

_____

Prayer

Lord, Let Your love shape my life with salvation and grace. Thank You for loving me through my darkest times. I'm desperate to hear from You and to walk in Your ways, not because I'm waiting on an answer, but because I truly love You. Amen.

Day 9
Hanging On for Dear Life

Today I will

- recognize the enduring power of God's love.
- create multiple ways to hold onto God's love.

Zayin

⁴⁹ Remember your promise to me;
it is my only hope.
⁵⁰ Your promise revives me;
it comforts me in all my troubles.
⁵¹ The proud hold me in utter contempt,
but I do not turn away from your instructions.
⁵² I meditate on your age-old regulations;
O Lord, they comfort me.
⁵³ I become furious with the wicked,
because they reject your instructions.
⁵⁴ Your decrees have been the theme of my songs
wherever I have lived.
⁵⁵ I reflect at night on who you are, O Lord;
therefore, I obey your instructions.
⁵⁶ This is how I spend my life:
obeying your commandments.

Psalm 119:49-56 NLT

Let's Talk about It

There's one truth that people don't often share about coping with difficulties in life: Our emotions toy with our ability to hope. When we are sad, anxious, hurt, or even fearful, our mind becomes clouded and we cannot see past our circumstances.

Even if we trust other people enough to admit our struggle to push through, their words can sometimes feel surface-level. They don't seem to permeate through the dark places within us that need the most care. As a result, their words don't sustain us.

That's why we need to hear from God Himself. When we read His words, there is a warmth that covers us for longer than just a moment. Hope is supernatural. Faith is supernatural. Therefore, when we are comforted to a point of feeling hope and faith amidst our troublesome circumstances and emotions, we experience the supernatural sustainability that only God can give. We can hardly describe it, but we can surely feel it.

There's an enduring power in God's words, too. The warmth we feel also comes through when we pray His words, sing His words, and even speak His words aloud. There's no magic happening here – just power from an everlasting God who has taken up residence in our hearts.

For that reason, we hang onto His every word—every promise, every command, and every chapter of His love story—because His words bring us back to life.

Day 9 Devotional

Digging Deeper

There are a number of creative ways to hold closely to God's word. It could be through the music you listen to, the prayers you speak, or even in your journal. (Sometimes, I even hang them on the wall and recite them when I pass by.) In what ways are you holding onto God's word? How do your current methods impact your hope and faith?

_____

_____

_____

_____

What are some other ways you could hold onto His words? List those out and create a plan of action to surround yourself in His promises even more.

_____

_____

_____

_____

Prayer

Lord, I reflect at night about who You are and how You love me. I pray, speak, and sing Your words back to You to demonstrate my agreement and challenge my own emotions. I pray that You continue to remind me of Your promises to sustain me through the night. Amen.

Day 10
Pure Devotion

Today I will

- identify ways I can show devotion to God, His word, and His followers.

Heth

⁵⁷ LORD, you are mine!
I promise to obey your words!
⁵⁸ With all my heart I want your blessings.
Be merciful as you promised.
⁵⁹ I pondered the direction of my life,
and I turned to follow your laws.
⁶⁰ I will hurry, without delay,
to obey your commands.
⁶¹ Evil people try to drag me into sin,
but I am firmly anchored to your instructions.
⁶² I rise at midnight to thank you
for your just regulations.
⁶³ I am a friend to anyone who fears you—
anyone who obeys your commandments.
⁶⁴ O LORD, your unfailing love fills the earth;
teach me your decrees.

Psalm 119:57-64 NLT

Let's Talk about It

As we grow in our relationship to God, it becomes more and more necessary to demonstrate our devotion to Him. In fact, showing our devotion becomes less of an effort—in time, we want to do it out of our love for Him.

Ultimately, our close relationship to God changes our hearts first. Then, it moves us towards a different, more promising way of living and being. Before we know it, the experience we have at midnight transforms us in our daylight, too.

Devotion comes in several forms. The psalmist talks about three of them:

1. Devotion to God: Continuously finding ways to be a friend to Him
2. Devotion to His word: Committing to understanding and following Him
3. Devotion to His followers: Finding ways to be God's hands and feet for others

One special result of our devotion to these is how it continues to shape and transform us. For example, actively pursuing a closer relationship with God increased my inner peace and decreased my frustrations. Adhering to God's words made me wiser in my decision making. Equally, serving others felt selfless and purposeful.

Following God is never boring. James 4:8 tells us that if we come close to God, He will come close to us (NLT). Therefore, make Him your constant pursuit.

Day 10 Devotional

Digging Deeper

Let's break down how to demonstrate devotion to God regularly. What ways can you devote yourself to your relationship to God?

_____
_____
_____

What ways can you devote yourself to God's words?

_____
_____
_____

What ways can you devote yourself to serving and loving His people?

_____
_____
_____

Prayer

Lord, I thank You for the opportunity to even get this close to You. I don't take it for granted, and I don't take You for granted. Please teach me how to show my devotion in all ways, at all times. Amen.

Day 11

The Start of a Breakthrough

Today I will

- recognize and acknowledge God's fulfilled promises to me.
- recognize my growth through this journey.

Teth

⁶⁵ *You have done many good things for me, Lord,*
just as you promised.
⁶⁶ *I believe in your commands;*
now teach me good judgment and knowledge.
⁶⁷ *I used to wander off until you disciplined me;*
but now I closely follow your word.
⁶⁸ *You are good and do only good;*
teach me your decrees.
⁶⁹ *Arrogant people smear me with lies,*
but in truth I obey your commandments with all my heart.
⁷⁰ *Their hearts are dull and stupid,*
but I delight in your instructions.
⁷¹ *My suffering was good for me,*
for it taught me to pay attention to your decrees.
⁷² *Your instructions are more valuable to me*
than millions in gold and silver.

Psalm 119:65-72 NLT

Let's Talk about It

Sometimes when we anticipate growth, we picture it being some sort of instantaneous occurrence: We're walking along one day and then BOOM—we are suddenly struck with growth. Sounds good, right? Maybe so, but you and I both know that it's never that easy or simplistic.

Growth happens over time. Day by day (and sometimes even hour by hour), we are changing through our thoughts, feelings, and actions as they evolve over time to more God-like responses. That BOOM happens when we one day recognize that our methods for handling difficult situations and people are vastly different than before.

While our first thought may be to give ourselves credit, we must remember that God gets all the glory, especially when bringing us out of our dark places.

To that end, think about the promises God has made to you. While you may not see everything come to pass right now, there are certainly portions of the promises that have been fulfilled. Whether that is a different way of navigating your issues or engaging with others, God's hand is at work in your life, making good things happen.

We never want to be void of gratitude to the God that redeems us and transforms us. After all, He wants to hear our praise. The psalmist gives good examples of how he stops and thanks God for the work He's doing in his life, even if it is the result of being disciplined.

When we come to God with thanksgiving and praise, we will continue to see Him move in a mighty way.

Day 11 Devotional

Digging Deeper

Today, take time out to evaluate your growth and promises fulfilled. Hold onto this list when you are feeling doubtful or are faced with more difficulty and burden. Name specific ways you've noticed growth within yourself since you began this journey.

_____

_____

_____

_____

What promises has God fulfilled? Even if the promises have not fully come to pass, what clues indicate that you are moving in the right direction?

_____

_____

_____

_____

Prayer

Dear God, I truly feel like Your child. You comfort me in my distress. You lead me where to go. I'm incredibly thankful for all You've done for me and are continuing to do to transform me. My words will never be enough, but they are my portion to You.

Thank You, Lord, for choosing me and loving me. Amen.

Day 12

Becoming a Vessel God can Use

Today I will

- identify ways to be a model for others.

Yodh

*⁷³ You made me; you created me.
Now give me the sense to follow your commands.
⁷⁴ May all who fear you find in me a cause for joy,
for I have put my hope in your word.
⁷⁵ I know, O LORD, that your regulations are fair;
you disciplined me because I needed it.
⁷⁶ Now let your unfailing love comfort me,
just as you promised me, your servant.
⁷⁷ Surround me with your tender mercies so I may live,
for your instructions are my delight.
⁷⁸ Bring disgrace upon the arrogant people who lied about me;
meanwhile, I will concentrate on your commandments.
⁷⁹ Let me be united with all who fear you,
with those who know your laws.
⁸⁰ May I be blameless in keeping your decrees;
then I will never be ashamed.*

Psalm 119:73-80 NLT

Let's Talk about It

In yesterday's devotion, I spoke about recognizing growth. It's amazing. Part of my own growth included being able to let others in on my journey. (Sometimes the enemy will isolate you from others to the point where you think no one else will understand. That's when you're most susceptible to his attacks in your mind.)

It's been difficult, but I must admit: it has been extremely rewarding to know God is using me to be a model for others going from breakdown to breakthrough. As many times as we pray for Him to reveal our purpose, being a positive example right now for others is one of the first steps for each of us. This here is confirmation that we are truly glorifying His name through the work He is doing within us and through us.

The growth that occurs on this journey can feel like tension. Sometimes, it even feels painful. As much as we try not to admit it, that uncomfortable growth is needed for us to move into our next season in life.

But guess what? There are some people in this world—in your world—who need that same type of growth. They need to know what it feels like to totally surrender to God's will the way you have. They also need to hear someone say, "Me, too."

Listen, all the discipline, the setbacks, and the dark moments are all for a perfect purpose that God has for you. I know it's not easy, but it will take vulnerability to allow God to use you for others. So, let go and let God use you as His vessel.

Day 12 Devotional

Digging Deeper

Sometimes being a vessel from God is much easier said than done. It takes the full removal of your own desires so that you can fully surrender to Him. In my own experience, I've realized that it is often a supernatural peace that God gives me in my weaknesses.

What supernatural things will you need from God in order for Him to use you as a model for others during this season in your life?

_____

_____

_____

_____

How has God already used you as a vessel?

_____

_____

_____

_____

Prayer

Dear God, thank You for using me, even in the most difficult seasons of my life. Thank You for providing opportunities for me to serve others and be examples for those who are seeking Your face. Through my weakness, Your grace is sufficient, and I ask that You teach me how to glorify Your name in my story of faith. Amen.

Day 13 and 14

Recap and Reflection

Psalm 119:41-80

Go back through this week's reading. Write down any new thoughts that come to mind to deepen your perspective and reflection that you've gained.

_____
_____
_____
_____

Digging Deeper

Is there something you need to dig deeper on this weekend? Explore the things you wrote down this week and see if more revelations come to mind.

_____
_____
_____
_____

Prayer

After going back through this week's readings, write a personal prayer to God. Thank Him for what He's done for you and confess to Him what you've been holding onto this week. Release it into His hands through your prayer.

_____

_____

_____

_____

_____

_____

A Serving of Healing

The title of Day 12's devotion was "Becoming a Vessel God can Use." When I first realized that God was pulling on my heart to serve others, I questioned its validity.

God, is this really what you're requiring of me right now? I asked Him in a prayer. *How can I possibly help someone else when I'm in such need right now? What do I have to give?*

God's apparent strategies for my healing and progression just didn't make sense in my natural mind, but I believe God has a sense of humor. He loves to watch our mouths drop in awe when we finally see our situation the way He sees it.

I want to emphasize a point I made to you on Day 12 because it is so important to the act of growing closer to God during your midnight experience: Part of your own healing and progression is to serve others. It's not merely a suggestion for a feel-good moment. It's a mandate from God.

When we are in our most difficult moments in life, our circumstances will cloud our focus. All of our attention will be fixed on our situation to the point where everything else becomes secondary. While this is a natural reaction to dealing with our own cir-

The Midnight Experience

cumstances, it actually is doing the opposite of what God wants during our time of need. Subconsciously, you are operating from a place of self-centeredness and feelings of being owed something different. It's prideful thinking at its finest.

Now, I'm sure you're not intentionally operating from pride in this manner, but that's how the enemy deceptively attacks your thoughts. During your times of distress, the enemy would love nothing more than to rock you to sleep with subtle thoughts of *why me?* or *why now?* After all, if left untamed, those thoughts he placed on your mind turn into deeper feelings of sorrow, which then lead to you acting the way you feel and think. It's a concoction that can only lead to more turmoil.

Instead, God wants you to hear His words and trust His judgment. He does that by proverbially pulling you out of the depths of your situation, your feelings, and your thoughts to focus your attention on something or someone else. When we can rise above our circumstances, we are able to operate from a clear mind. God can surely use you then.

Jesus' entire life was literally a perfect example of serving others. Throughout the New Testament, the Bible indicates that Jesus was always aware of His purpose to go to the cross and be crucified to save humanity from their sins. I don't know about you, but if I knew my days were numbered, I wouldn't be in the best of moods. I would probably spend most of my time trying to convince God to change His mind or give me a different option. I'd be so focused on what was to come that I wouldn't be able to give my best self to others who need me most. I may even repeatedly ask God why this is happening to me. But Jesus spent the majority of His life healing and teaching others. He didn't complain about it, and He didn't fight against it. Even when He prayed for God to intervene during His final hours, He still wanted God's will to be done over anything else.

"He walked away, about a stone's throw, and knelt down and prayed, 'Father, if you are willing, please take this cup of suffering away from me. Yet I want your will to be done, not mine'" (Luke 22:41-42 NLT).

Jesus wasn't operating out of pride in that moment; He was operating from a place of obedience and trust. When you know and understand your purpose, you can always lean back on it.

Serving others will look different for everyone. You may feel like God is calling you to do more volunteering at church or in community organizations. You may feel as if God is compelling you to spend more time with an individual with whom you can encourage and share your own story. During my midnight experience, God gave me the ability to serve others in ways that I wouldn't have otherwise done. Let me tell you about three of them.

The Story of Kendra

I met Kendra through a mutual friend at church. I didn't know her too well, but I saw her every Sunday and during weekly church-related events. She was dating a man who also attended our church and everyone knew they were quite serious.

After two years, Kendra and the guy ended their relationship. She was very much heartbroken, and I even saw her crying a few times during a church service. For reasons that only God could explain, I really felt compassion for her while she was going through this and could tell she was having a tough time moving forward. I decided to approach her one day after church to encourage her about life after a breakup, something I recently experienced myself. We talked for so long that we agreed to continue meeting up for about two more months.

Kendra and I would meet for coffee at a local shop. During those times, she would pour out her heart to me and talk about how she was working on herself. From our conversations, I was continuously surprised by how much I could relate to her! Our personal stories were very similar, which compelled me even more to encourage her through my own walk with God. At the same time, I felt like God was shaping my perspective by having me look at my own reflection through her story.

The Story of Ministering to the Homeless

I volunteered with a particular church ministry for over four years. This particular ministry aimed to serve the homeless community in a more personal way. So, each Sunday the church would send a shuttle bus to pick up a group of people from two local homeless shelters and bring them to our church. During their time with us, we would have the opportunity to serve them breakfast, fellowship with them, and share a twenty-minute encouraging message with them before they attended the church service with us. Volunteering for this ministry was the highlight of my week and I knew it was the same for others.

One weekend, the leader of this church ministry asked me to deliver the devotional message for the upcoming weekend. I was so honored, nervous, and excited all at the same time. I spent the days leading up to it praying, seeking insight, and preparing for a message that would be relevant and useful to our homeless guests.

When the day finally arrived, I delivered a message about how Jesus was already in the process of working things out in our situation, even if we could not yet see Him. I chose that message because I felt as if that was the one God laid on my heart as the most relevant to the people in the room. It was just a relevant to my own life. And while some of the guests shared how much they appreciated my words, there were two women who volunteered alongside me each week who were visibly moved by my message of hope. During our discussion time, they both shared with the group about how relevant my message was to their current circumstances. Through their tears, they also explained how this was exactly what they needed to hear that day. I was stunned, not because of the powerful message I just delivered, but because of the powerful God who knew exactly what I should say to impact those who needed it most. God prepared for me to be a blessing to my fellow volunteers that morning and I didn't even know it.

The Story of Joshua

Joshua and I met at a previous work event. In the midst of talking about job-related topics, our conversation evolved into the topic of dealing with mental illness. During that time, Joshua confided in me about his struggles with obsessive–compulsive disorder and how it was an ongoing fight for his sanity. I encouraged him to read a blog post that I once wrote about dealing with depression. Once he read it, our conversation and connection increased. Although I didn't know much about obsessive-compulsive disorder, I was empathetic to his struggles and wanted to encourage him to find God's peace through it all. The more we talked, the more I saw similarities in our pursuit of peace.

One day, I was having a particularly hard time. I just received some news that really hurt me and made me fall deeper into sadness. I cried out to God for mercy, strength and peace, wondering how I could ever get beyond this dark place. Then, something miraculous happened: In the middle of my tears, Joshua called me.

This certainly wasn't a planned conversation for either of us. Joshua told me he wasn't going to call, but he really felt like it was the right thing to do because he needed someone to talk to and someone to pray for him. He told me that he was having a particularly hard time that day dealing with his disorder and that he felt like he was falling into deep sadness. (Yes, he used those same exact words.) In fact, some of the very things I had *just* said to God in my prayer came out of his mouth on the phone regarding his own feelings! I was absolutely stunned, and all I could do was cry in disbelief. I knew God was at work in that moment. I prayed with Joshua over the phone, but I knew that God was using my own words to comfort me in that moment, too.

By serving Kendra through supportive conversations and a listening ear, I was mentally and spiritually opened to an understanding of my own journey, even much more. By faithfully serving on a ministry team at church, God gave me the privilege of ministering to others who needed to hear His voice. By my acts of service to Joshua through prayer and encouragement, I also encouraged myself during a difficult time. God really does work in mysterious ways and He's using every opportunity for a blessing in your life and the life of others.

The Midnight Experience

This week you saw that the psalmist prayed for God to send His mercy and comfort him with His unfailing love. While he doesn't get specific about how God actually blesses him with what he asks for, we can safely assume that God did indeed respond. The Bible says in Matthew 7:7 that if we ask it, we shall receive it (NLT). It's important to understand that when God gives, it usually won't look the way we are expecting it to be. That comfort, mercy, and unfailing love just may appear through our service to others.

So be sure that you maintain an open heart and open mind during your midnight experience. This will create room for God to bring miracles to your life, even while He is using you to be a miracle in another's life.

Section Three

Day Fifteen through Day Twenty-One

What's in the Eye of Your Storm?

Before proceeding, let's do a recap of where we've been. At the beginning of this book, I set the scene for you. I shared what was occurring and why you may be experiencing a midnight experience at this point in your life. It was necessary that you got yourself in position to hear God's voice before proceeding forward.

Then, you walked through the concept of your deepest needs and why God was and is the only One who can meet them. After all, He is the One who placed them within you. From there, I explained the difference between what the world defines as love versus what God created love to be. I'm sure you heard before that *God is love*, and hopefully by now, you can understand why. Finally, I shared my personal stories about how serving others can actually serve *you*.

From where we've been, there is a key concept about your midnight experience that you must understand: While you're waiting on God's promises, He is taking you on a journey to newness. Here are two scriptures in the Bible that really emphasize the very essence of how God works:

> "Look, I am about to do something new; even now it is coming. Do you not see it? Indeed, I will make a way in the wilderness, rivers in the desert" (Isaiah 43:19 HCSB).

> "Don't copy the behavior and customs of this world, but let God transform you into a new person by changing the way you think. Then you will learn to know God's will for you, which is good and pleasing and perfect" (Romans 12:2 NLT).

All of this is to prepare you for what He has in store for you. You can't step into God's new promises with old habits and ways of thinking because you won't last long. You won't be able to handle what He's giving to you. That's a paradox, and it just doesn't make sense.

It sounds simple enough, right? One would think that a simple how-to manual would be enough for your encounter with God, but it's not that easy. There are forces at play that are not excited about your growing relationship with God. Those evil forces are doing everything they can to get you off track of where God is trying to take you. They see the promises He has in store for you, and they're working to distract you from it. One of the most common ways the enemy does this is through fear tactics. Once you hit your midnight hour—also known as the middle of the night—that is when it gets interesting. You've likely stepped into the middle of your fears, frustrations, confusions, doubts, and sorrow. It's the eye of the storm that you were hoping to never see.

The Eye of the Storm

Every tropical cyclone has an eye in the middle of the storm. The eye forms when wind speeds increase to 80 miles per hour or more. Within this eye, the weather is most calm and stable. Many times, the rain has ceased and there may even be a bright spot in the sky.

While the atmosphere appears at peace, one mustn't be fooled. The ceased rain is a false harmony. What it actually means is that the storm is halfway over and more turmoil is to come. Meteorologists often emphasize the eye of the storm because they are warning their viewing audience that trouble is ahead.

That danger is primarily found around the eye of the storm, called the eyewall. The eyewall encircles the actual eye with a round of tumultuous winds and weighted thunderstorms. Anyone who knows storms knows that this is the most destructive part of it, especially when the winds are moving in the same direction as the storm's forward motion.

Let's think about this for a moment. When storms appear in our lives, do they not feel the same way? We experience troubling moments of the storm and once the calm occurs, we are desperately hoping that our storm is over. But many times, our biggest fear comes to life when we realize that the worst is yet to come. Amidst the middle of our storms, we see the chaotic winds of doubt, fear, and sorrow (among many other negative emotions) surround us. We feel trapped. We feel confused. We wonder if we'll ever make it out.

It's during your midnight storm that we become the most mentally fatigued. This is when our mind plays tricks on us and we question what we were once confident in. The enemy likes it when we tire out like this because we can more easily step into his playground without even realizing it. So how do you know when you're in the devil's playground? Let's take a look at Jesus' own midnight experience for clues.

Each of the gospel accounts shares the story of Jesus being led by the Holy Spirit into the wilderness to be tempted by Satan. (More about the Divine's role in our difficult times later.) This wasn't a deceitful trick that the Holy Spirit was doing; rather, this was a test of Jesus' commitment to His Father and His purpose. The Bible shares that during the forty days and forty nights that Jesus was alone in the wilderness, Satan came out to play with the root of Jesus' motives.

¹Then Jesus was led by the Spirit into the wilderness to be tempted there by the devil. ² For forty days and forty nights he fasted and became very hungry. ³During that time the devil came and said to him, "If you are the

Son of God, tell these stones to become loaves of bread." ⁴But Jesus told him, "No! The Scriptures say, 'People do not live by bread alone, but by every word that comes from the mouth of God.'" ⁵Then the devil took him to the holy city, Jerusalem, to the highest point of the Temple, ⁶and said, "If you are the Son of God, jump off! For the Scriptures say, 'He will order his angels to protect you. And they will hold you up with their hands so you won't even hurt your foot on a stone.'" ⁷Jesus responded, "The Scriptures also say, 'You must not test the Lord your God.'" ⁸Next the devil took him to the peak of a very high mountain and showed him all the kingdoms of the world and their glory. ⁹"I will give it all to you," he said, "if you will kneel down and worship me." ¹⁰"Get out of here, Satan," Jesus told him. "For the Scriptures say, 'You must worship the Lord your God and serve only him.'" ¹¹Then the devil went away, and angels came and took care of Jesus (Matthew 4:1-11 NLT).

We have to assume that this was when Jesus was at His lowest. He was hungry, He was tired, and had been at this place for a really long time without human contact. He could've easily fallen into one of the devil's traps. It almost would've made sense for Him to do so, but He didn't.

The devil tried three different times to provoke Jesus. In order to fully grasp how it connects to our own life, let's break down each one.

The Temptation of Impatience

"During that time the devil came and said to him, 'If you are the Son of God, tell these stones to become loaves of bread'" (Matthew 4:3 NLT).

First, the devil tempted Jesus with impatience. Do you ever notice that when you desire something, that feeling gradually increases until the need is met? This is what the devil was hoping would occur with Jesus because He hadn't eaten in so long. If left untamed, it will become easier to fall forward into one's desire without stopping to consider the consequences of not waiting on God. Think about it: Wasn't God fully aware that Jesus was hungry? God knew Jesus' state of being in that moment but was teaching Him to feed His desires on greater things. If we believe that God is a loving and faithful God, we must trust that God has a bigger plan and would provide for us when the time is right.

The same is true in our own situations. Waiting on His promise can seem like an eternity in our natural minds; however, we must continue to trust that God has a reason for everything He does, and He will deliver His promises at the right time. If you pick grapes too early, they will have negative consequences on the wine you're intending to make. In the same way, if we try to attain our promise too early, we can interrupt what God already has in store.

The Temptation of Doubt

"Then the devil took him to the holy city, Jerusalem, to the highest point of the Temple, ⁶ and said, "If you are the Son of God, jump off! For the Scriptures say,

*'He will order his angels to protect you.
And they will hold you up with their hands
so you won't even hurt your foot on a stone'"* (Matthew 4:5-6 NLT).

The second temptation that the devil uses is doubt. In this passage, he was working hard at convincing Jesus to question God's promises. If Jesus had jumped in that moment, His actions would have meant that He really didn't trust God's words after all. But testing God does not make Him move any faster. This is not what God wants from us. We are to trust His words fully because He spoke them and has yet to fail us.

During seasons such as this, it can be easy for us to say things such as "Maybe I didn't hear God correctly" or "Maybe God forgot about me." We can even wonder if we sinned one too many times and the delay is God's way of changing His mind. Resist the temptation to question God. If He said it, He meant it. It *will* come to pass. It will.

The Temptation of Pride

Next the devil took him to the peak of a very high mountain and showed him all the kingdoms of the world and their glory. "I will give it all to you," he said, "if you will kneel down and worship me" (Matthew 4:8-9 NLT).

Finally, the devil tempted Jesus with His own pride. I think it's pretty profound that Satan showed Jesus what *all* could be His if He only gave him His worship. Our worship doesn't belong to anyone else but to God, and this passage teaches us that. But when our fleshly desires become so strong that they start to take over our rational thinking, it makes it that much easier to submit to something or someone other than God.

Jesus could have very well felt that He *deserved* all of the kingdoms of the world at that very moment and submitted to the devil's "promise" rather than waiting on God's. But understand this: Whatever is unaligned to God's word is not from Him. Regardless of how heavy our storms, regardless of how chaotic the eyewall is around us, we must always know the difference between what God's word is and what it is not. That is why it's so important to study the Bible—His living word. Jesus knew what God *already* promised Him. His Kingdom would be greater than anything the devil offered in that moment. Therefore, there was no reason to waiver.

When we are waiting on God's promises, we can expect that storms will be a part of our midnight experience. Nowhere in the Bible does God say that our journey will come without difficulty; in fact, He may even allow some of that difficulty to create discipline inside of us as we build our faith and become more like Him. While knowing that may be encouraging, it doesn't make our circumstances hurt any less.

I want to bring something back to your attention. I told you earlier that I'd share more about the Divine's role during your difficult times. Know that it's not a misprint in the Bible when it says that the Holy Spirit led Jesus into the wilderness to be tempted. While Jesus was being tempted, God was in control the entire time.

What's in the Eye of Your Storm?

When you are a child of the Most High, everything that occurs in your life has to go through His hands. He knows what's occurring, and He has a God-size reason for allowing it, which He'll eventually reveal to you. As I mentioned before, Jesus' wilderness experience acted as a training ground for His calling and His commitment. Your midnight experience is your training ground, too. So there's no need to be afraid even in your darkest of nights. God is there and He is still in control.

The upcoming devotions are very telling about what the psalmist is experiencing during the storms of his life. From the questions he asks to the complaints that he makes, it is evident that he, too, is in the middle of his journey. As you proceed in your reading, you'll see that his tone changes as he eventually rises out of his difficult moments to praise God's word once again. His many waves of emotions throughout the psalms are all too real.

Like the psalmist, it is normal to have a full range of emotions during this time in your life. No one is denying that. But being here is about recognizing what's occurring and trusting God to move you through it. As you will see from the psalmist, *choosing* to rely on God only increased his faith. His strength came from the truth of the Word, not the thickness of the night and not even from the strength of his enemies.

In the middle of our storms is where the rubber meets the road. You now have a choice to make: Will you succumb to the eyewall of fear, doubt, jealousy, sorrow, and anxiety that is circulating around you or will you stand above your circumstance to remember the truth that lies in the word of God? Believe me when I say that this is indeed a difficult decision, and not everyone chooses wisely. Allow me to say it one more time: This is your training ground for God to bring you to your promise. Trust that He is in control and knows exactly what He's doing even when you don't.

As you proceed with your next set of devotions, consider what is occurring around you. Are you in the eye of your storm or the eyewall? What is your eyewall filled with? What does that mean for your level of worship, prayer, and faith? Even if you're in a pretty good place right now emotionally, it's helpful to recognize the signs of what is to come. While we can't always forecast bad weather, we always know that darkness is on its way at some point in the future. Do yourself a favor and proceed with caution.

Day 15

The Five W's of Waiting

Today I will

- commit to trusting God in the middle of my storm.

Kaph

⁸¹ I am worn out waiting for your rescue,
but I have put my hope in your word.
⁸² My eyes are straining to see your promises come true.
When will you comfort me?
⁸³ I am shriveled like a wineskin in the smoke,
but I have not forgotten to obey your decrees.
⁸⁴ How long must I wait?
When will you punish those who persecute me?
⁸⁵ These arrogant people who hate your instructions
have dug deep pits to trap me.
⁸⁶ All your commands are trustworthy.
Protect me from those who hunt me down without cause.
⁸⁷ They almost finished me off,
but I refused to abandon your commandments.
⁸⁸ In your unfailing love, spare my life;
then I can continue to obey your laws.

Psalm 119:81-88 NLT

Let's Talk about It

God, I'm worn out waiting for Your rescue. I know those words of the psalmist all too well. What I found to be true is that while we may struggle to maintain focus daily through this experience, we become even more desperate in the middle of our storm.

In the middle. It seems like the storm hits us the hardest in the middle, and since we've reached the middle of our 30 days of devotion, it all makes sense. It's during these times that our eyes begin to strain, our bones begin to ache, and we are eons away from a resolution to our circumstance. We are desperate. God knows it, and so does the enemy.

In the middle, we have a decision to make: We consider stopping the fight right here and going back to the way things were. But, we remember what we left back there and realize it's not where we want to return. We also look ahead for a glimpse of hope, but we're quickly discouraged because we can't see the light. We don't even know how much further we have to go.

So, we remain where we are while asking God one or all of the five W's:

Who am I anymore?
What do I do in this moment?
When will You rescue me?
Where will my breakthrough come from?
Why is this happening to me? To ME?!

I believe that in the middle of our questions and our storm, God has one question for us: How deep is your faith?

God knows about the storm you're facing. He sees it. Just because it's getting harder doesn't mean He's not at work. Believe in faith that He's got you and He's working all things out for the "good of those who love Him and are called according to His purpose" (Romans 8:28 NKJV).

Day 15 Devotional

Digging Deeper

During my most desperate times is when I am most honest with God. Sometimes it hurts to even speak the words out loud, but if there is anyone to be honest with, God is that One. Be honest with Him today. Talk to Him and share your deepest worries, fears, frustrations, and cries. Let Him hear You. Allow Him to carry you through. You can start by writing them down.

_____
_____
_____
_____
_____
_____

Prayer

Lord, I know You see what's happening in my world. This internal pain is getting heavy and I'm desperate for a breakthrough. Give me grace, God, as I continue to follow Your words. Your will be done in this moment. Please, get me through this. Amen.

Day 16

Silencing the Enemy

Today I will

- identify ways to silence the negativity and focus on God's faithfulness.

Lamedh

⁸⁹ Your eternal word, O LORD,
stands firm in heaven.
⁹⁰ Your faithfulness extends to every generation,
as enduring as the earth you created.
⁹¹ Your regulations remain true to this day,
for everything serves your plans.
⁹² If your instructions hadn't sustained me with joy,
I would have died in my misery.
⁹³ I will never forget your commandments,
for by them you give me life.
⁹⁴ I am yours; rescue me!
For I have worked hard at obeying your commandments.
⁹⁵ Though the wicked hide along the way to kill me,
I will quietly keep my mind on your laws.
⁹⁶ Even perfection has its limits,
but your commands have no limit.

Psalm 119:89-96 NLT

Let's Talk about It

What if all we had to do on this earth was trust God without an opposing option? What if there were no enemies to distract us or tempt us? I don't know about you, but that would make this journey so much easier for me.

Unfortunately, that's not the case in this current life. We are dealing with an enemy who finds joy in separating us from God, because he knows he can never get God to separate from us. For that reason, we must stand firm on God's words. As mentioned earlier, it's our only hope.

Keep in mind that the closer you draw to God, and the more you trust His words, the more the enemy will come in for the attack. And one of the most harmful weapons he uses against us is our own thoughts. The battleground is your mind.

If we're going to stay on this journey and go the distance, it is necessary for us to work on what we're thinking about and even how long we think about it. If not, we'll find ourselves in a labyrinth of mental chaos filled with doubt and ultimate separation from the relationship we're working so hard to grow.

It's time to fight back with focus and determination. Whenever you feel clouded with negative thoughts of doubt, fear, frustration, or just plain sadness, pray. Pray to God to change your thoughts because you know that it's of the enemy, not of God. This is easier said than done, but once you do it, you'll feel more empowered than ever before. Focus your thoughts on His faithfulness, not your circumstances.

Day 16 Devotional

Digging Deeper

There are a number of ways to control your thoughts and focus on what you want to focus on. Some people use exercise such as yoga to help. Some even engage in meditation regularly. While those are all good strategies, the simplest and most direct way to shift your thoughts to God's words is through prayer using His words (scriptures). Try it, and see how it quickly transforms you from a state of negativity to a state of peace.

Write a prayer that speaks God's own words over your life. During your next episode, pray that prayer out loud—repeatedly if you have to.

_____
_____
_____
_____
_____

Prayer

Lord, I'm so thankful that Your words are eternal, regardless of where I am, where I've been, or where I'm going. I pray that You help me to control what the enemy places in my mind. If it weren't for You, I'd be in utter misery. Keep me focused on You, God, as I speak Your words over my life and focus on Your faithfulness. Amen.

Day 17

Prison Break

Today I will

- identify clear examples of how my devotion to God and His word has turned to love.

Mem

^{97} Oh, how I love your instructions!
I think about them all day long.
^{98} Your commands make me wiser than my enemies,
for they are my constant guide.
^{99} Yes, I have more insight than my teachers,
for I am always thinking of your laws.
^{100} I am even wiser than my elders,
for I have kept your commandments.
^{101} I have refused to walk on any evil path,
so that I may remain obedient to your word.
^{102} I haven't turned away from your regulations,
for you have taught me well.
^{103} How sweet your words taste to me;
they are sweeter than honey.
^{104} Your commandments give me understanding;
no wonder I hate every false way of life.

Psalm 119:97-104 NLT

Let's Talk about It

"How do I love thee? Let me count the ways.[4]"

The first line of this famous sonnet by Elizabeth Barrett Browning is so fitting with the psalmist's words today. Reading these verses, one can't deny how much he adores God's words, so much so that he breaks it down into examples of how it has changed him. While he doesn't say that obeying God has taken away his enemies, he does say it has changed how he thinks and how he chooses to respond to others.

It's important for us to consider our own love for God's word in a way that's tangible. This is not only beneficial for our own awareness, but it is also helpful as God uses us to help or encourage others.

Here are some important questions for you to ask yourself as you ponder the thought of your love for God's word:

- How many times has God's word comforted you?
- How have your thoughts and motivations changed since devoting yourself to God's word?
- What do you believe now about the power of God's word in your life and circumstances?

Being able to answer these questions is a great start because it focuses your attention on what's going well in your life versus what is not. The more I've done this in my own life, the more I realize some other truths

One more important thought on this: Celebrating your love for God's word shuts down the enemy's attacks. He hates to hear our praise because it means he's losing this fight for your soul. So keep celebrating, and keep winning!

Day 17 Devotional

Digging Deeper

Today, I encourage you to expand even more on the three bullet points above. Celebrate your growth and your love for God's word. It can't be denied, and definitely shouldn't be silenced.

_____

_____

_____

_____

_____

_____

Prayer

Dear God, I thank You for the opportunity to immerse myself in Your word daily. It's changing me. It's healing me. You make me brave against my enemy, and for that, I am eternally changed.

Continue to draw near to me as I continue to do the same. Amen.

Day 18

Declare It to Your Soul

Today I will

- declare God's promises over my life.

Nun

*105 Your word is a lamp to guide my feet
and a light for my path.
106 I've promised it once, and I'll promise it again:
I will obey your righteous regulations.
107 I have suffered much, O Lord;
restore my life again as you promised.
108 Lord, accept my offering of praise,
and teach me your regulations.
109 My life constantly hangs in the balance,
but I will not stop obeying your instructions.
110 The wicked have set their traps for me,
but I will not turn from your commandments.
111 Your laws are my treasure;
they are my heart's delight.
112 I am determined to keep your decrees
to the very end.*

Psalm 119:105-112 NLT

Let's Talk about It

It's not fair: Sometimes it seems like as soon as we feel better, we are back to our dark place at midnight. What gives? It's just—not—fair.

Unfortunately, that's how life works. As much as we try, we feel like we can't catch a break. That was the story of my life for months. I felt like I was just trying to make it from day to day, hour to hour even. Although I was faithful in obedience to God, there were still dark skies that would hover over me during my most vulnerable moments. I thought I was actually going crazy.

But here's the truth that gave me comfort: Because I had stored God's words down in my heart, I could declare them over my life whenever I needed and wanted. Similarly, God would remind me of His words when I cried out to Him for help.

I'm sure you realize by now that attacks will still raid and storms will still blow. I said it before and I'll say it again: the enemy is trying to separate you from your Savior. But, when we remain close to God, He promises to stay close to us and walk with us through our trials.

Stand firm in what you know to be true about the God who calls you His own child. Declare His words over your life and watch the enemy flee!

Day 18 Devotional

Digging Deeper

One of the most healing moments of my midnight experiences was when I learned to declare God's words over my life. With all the promises that He gives in the Bible, we need to speak them, pray them, and proclaim our faith in them. His words are transformational, and they will transform the way you maneuver through your struggles.

Which of God's promises do you need to declare over your life? Write them down and begin to say them out loud whenever you feel necessary. You may even schedule times to say them, such as morning, noon, and before bed.

_____

_____

_____

_____

Prayer

Dear God, thank You for ultimate access to Your word. Your words comfort me. As I think of which promises to speak over my life when I'm down, I pray that You bring to my mind your sacred, loving words. Amen.

Day 19

God's Power vs. Man's Power

Today I will

- ask God for His supernatural strength to carry me through.

Samekh

¹¹³ I hate those with divided loyalties,
but I love your instructions.
¹¹⁴ You are my refuge and my shield;
your word is my source of hope.
¹¹⁵ Get out of my life, you evil-minded people,
for I intend to obey the commands of my God.
¹¹⁶ LORD, sustain me as you promised, that I may live!
Do not let my hope be crushed.
¹¹⁷ Sustain me, and I will be rescued;
then I will meditate continually on your decrees.
¹¹⁸ But you have rejected all who stray from your decrees.
They are only fooling themselves.
¹¹⁹ You skim off the wicked of the earth like scum;
no wonder I love to obey your laws!
¹²⁰ I tremble in fear of you;
I stand in awe of your regulations.

Psalm 119:113-120 NLT

Let's Talk about It

Do you ever feel like you are praying for the same things? Sometimes, I get so tired of hearing my own words over and over, especially when my circumstance is still the same. Today's devotion comes from several things we've discussed up to this point:

- Loving God's words
- Seeking a solution for dealing with enemies
- Seeking supernatural intervention

At this point, you already know what to do: Continue to pray, worship, and speak God's word over your life. But there comes a time—and this may very well be that time—when you need God's supernatural strength to get you through this tough time.

There are countless stories in the Bible that defend this idea: People try to use their own strength and wisdom to handle issues. God proves over and over again that God-size issues are meant for God-size power and authority. Some things just weren't meant for us to figure out. That's why we come from a God who is greater than anything and anyone we face. Our part is to ask with sincerity and believe in faith that God will provide for us. The more we seek Him, the less we are afraid to enter the next midnight.

Day 19 Devotional

Digging Deeper

What kind of supernatural power do you need from God? Some things that many people ask for are peace, patience, wisdom, and comfort.

_____
_____
_____
_____

Spend time today asking God for what you specifically need. His word says He promises to provide, if only you ask.

_____
_____
_____
_____

Prayer

Dear God, there comes a time when I have to admit my weakness, and I'm now ready to come to terms with that. I can't do any of this on my own strength. I've proven that. I need what only You can give. Take over, God, and restore me back to what's better than this. Amen.

Day 20 and 21

Recap and Reflection

Psalm 119:81-120

Go back through this week's reading. Write down any new thoughts that come to mind to deepen your perspective and reflection that you've gained.

_____
_____
_____
_____

Digging Deeper

Is there something you need to dig deeper on this weekend? Explore the things you wrote down this week and see if more revelations come to mind.

_____
_____
_____
_____

Prayer

After going back through this week's readings, write a personal prayer to God. Thank Him for what He's done for you and confess to Him what you've been holding onto this week. Release it into His hands through your prayer.

_____

_____

_____

_____

_____

_____

Confessions to the One Who already Knows

Nathan was in a particularly difficult season of his life. He felt as though God called him into ministry, but nothing about his life indicated that this is what was in store for him. He was asked to volunteer in what could be considered mundane activities at church, such as cleaning up each week after the services and passing out flyers. Instead, he wanted someone to give him the opportunity to refine his communication and presentation skills on a platform—with a large Bible and a large audience.

Not only that, Nathan had a negative attitude every time he clocked in to his day job. He felt as if his supervisor and colleagues didn't recognize his talent and, therefore, struggled to see the value and purpose in his work there. He was waiting for his supervisor to give him more leadership opportunities and a promotion, but neither ever came.

Eventually, Nathan worked himself into deep frustration. He wanted so badly to fulfill God's will for his life, but couldn't understand why it wasn't coming to fruition around him. With every stumbling block that came his way, he began to lose hope in what

God promised him, wondering if he even heard Him correctly. This soon made him angry at his circumstances.

One morning, during his Bible reading and devotion time, Nathan became overwhelmed with emotion and cried out to God in prayer about his anger. For the first time, he spoke out loud to Him about the entire situation. He admitted to what he originally expected and why he was upset. He asked God for confirmation that His promise was true and would still come to pass. What He spoke back to Nathan completely caught him off guard.

In His loving response, God led him to scriptures that spoke about pride. He told Nathan that pride was permeating his heart and that was why he was stagnant in his progression. God also told him that within his current responsibilities at church and his job, He was teaching him about humility and servanthood. Until he learned those lessons, he would never see ministry opportunities come to pass because he wouldn't be able to endure the mindsets that were required.

In spite of the tough love, God revealed to Nathan that he was indeed fulfilling His will for his life right now, which was to be still at church and work. He was right where he was supposed to be, and He was working it all out to prepare Nathan for his next season. From that day forward, Nathan had a totally different outlook on his life and worked to change his misguided expectations.

Before Nathan could move forward, he had to get honest with himself and with God. In just one encounter, God's words spoke more to him than anything he could've come up with on his own. It changed his entire way of thinking and his approach to his circumstances. That, my friend, is transformation at its finest.

One thing believers should appreciate about God is that He will never force Himself or His will on anyone. So it's often up to us to call on God to seek His counsel. When we do, He will tell us everything we need to know to move us forward.

Throughout Psalm 119, we can appreciate how honest the psalmist was with God. Whenever he was joyful, thankful, or awestruck with God's goodness, he verbalized it. There was never a time in his prayers to God that we weren't certain of how happy he was about Him. Even when he was down, he still showed gratitude and love towards the One who could change his circumstances.

When the psalmist was fearful, doubtful, or angry, he admitted that as well. There are times when it seemed like he was experiencing a rollercoaster of emotion and gave it all to God. Maybe that's true, but is that a bad thing? I mean, who else loves you enough to ride the wave with you like the One who created you?

What I've come to realize is that many Christians shy away from just being plain honest with God, particularly when it comes to sharing hurts, frustrations, fears, and anger. Why is that? Do we think that God cannot handle our messy, raw emotions? On the contrary, God actually *wants* us to be honest with Him. It's within that honesty that God can break through our limited perspective and get us to see things through His spiritual eyes. If Nathan hadn't come to God with his unfiltered feelings, he would've sat much longer with the belief that his lack of progress was everyone else's fault. In his confession, God awakened his spiritual eyes to see things from His point of view. His spiritual eyes trump our natural eyes every time.

Another reason we should be honest with God is that He already knows what we're wrestling with in our heart. God is the only One who knows how deep our hurt goes. He's the only One who has seen every piece of the story we carry around. He's the omniscient, omnipresent God and He walks with us every day. Confessing your deepest feelings ultimately gets us into alignment with Him so that we *can* have an encounter.

Let me be clear that what I'm suggesting to you is to confess to God, not to complain to Him. Those are two entirely different things. When you confess what's on your heart, you are sharing what you are feeling. You're stating facts about how you perceive your present situation and following up with seeking His explanation. When you complain, you are giving an opinion about how you perceive your situation and taking it as fact. The major difference is that complaining is rooted in pride. When we gripe about what's not going the way *we* think it should go, we are ultimately telling God we have a better plan than His. Complaining is not useful in the natural world, and it certainly not useful in the spiritual world, either.

It matters how you, bring your stuff to God. He loves you unconditionally, but He does not love a complaining spirit. This was especially evident in the story of the Israelites.

Earlier in this book, I talked about the Israelites learning how to fully depend on God for their deepest needs. Those same Israelites who were taught many lessons also complained heavily along the way. To us readers, they seem completely ungrateful and irrational.

There was a time when the Israelites were about to cross the Jordan to enter into the Promised Land that God spoke of. To prepare, God told Moses to send twelve spies to scope out the land and report back their findings. When those twelve men returned, ten of them made it seem as if the inhabitants of the land were larger than life and would cause more trouble than a blessing for the Israelites. (Clearly, they were viewing this situation through their natural eyes rather than spiritual.) The Israelites took this as an opportunity to complain and grumble:

> *"¹Then the whole community began weeping aloud, and they cried all night. ²Their voices rose in a great chorus of protest against Moses and Aaron. 'If only we had died in Egypt, or even here in the wilderness!' they complained. ³'Why is the Lord taking us to this country only to have us die in battle? Our wives and our little ones will be carried off as plunder! Wouldn't it be better for us to return to Egypt?' ⁴Then they plotted among themselves, 'Let's choose a new leader and go back to Egypt!'"* (Numbers 14:1-4 NLT)

Instead of getting what they wanted sooner, their complaining actually stalled their progress. God punished them with forty more years in the wilderness and told them that those who complained would never see the Promised Land.

I share this illustration not to threaten you, but to further emphasize the difference between confessions and complaining. If the Israelites had approached God with a purer heart that demonstrated their ultimate trust in Him rather than their doubt, God might have responded differently. There are plenty of examples in the Bible where He did. But the lesson to be learned here is that God will move when our heart's intentions are right. The psalmist's words, as we've already read, are a great example of this as well. He inquired, confessed, and still praised God all in the same breath.

Ultimately, this is all about releasing your deep emotions so that God can deal with them, whether that be to show you a different perspective or to heal you. In the next section, we'll talk about the healing power of speaking God's words back to Him. I have found that verbally releasing His words can start the engine for growth. That growth places you on the path toward receiving His promises.

Section Four

Day Twenty-Two through Day Twenty-Eight

Speak Your Life into Existence

Everything you've read up to this point has been purposeful in your understanding of the journey you're on while waiting for God's promises. I've even given you action steps here and there to help you continue moving forward. Now, I want to talk to you about something that is often overlooked among believers, but comes directly from God's Word. Out of all the other points I've discussed, this section is by far the biggest charge you'll have for your journey and your life.

Let's start with Genesis 1 and portions of Genesis 2. It's a lengthy text, the most scripture you've read in this book, but I encourage you to read them thoroughly for context of the rest of this chapter. I'll meet you at the end of the scriptures.

The Story of Creation

[1]*In the beginning God created the heavens and the earth.* [2]*The earth was without form, and void; and darkness was on the face of the deep. And the Spirit of God was hovering over the face of the waters.*

The Midnight Experience

³Then God said, "Let there be light"; and there was light. ⁴And God saw the light that it was good; and God divided the light from the darkness. ⁵God called the light Day, and the darkness He called Night. So the evening and the morning were the first day.

⁶Then God said, "Let there be a firmament in the midst of the waters, and let it divide the waters from the waters." ⁷Thus God made the firmament, and divided the waters which were under the firmament from the waters which were above the firmament; and it was so. ⁸And God called the firmament Heaven. So the evening and the morning were the second day.

⁹Then God said, "Let the waters under the heavens be gathered together into one place, and let the dry land appear;" and it was so. ¹⁰And God called the dry land Earth, and the gathering together of the waters He called Seas. And God saw that it was good.

¹¹Then God said, "Let the earth bring forth grass, the herb that yields seed, and the fruit tree that yields fruit according to its kind, whose seed is in itself, on the earth"; and it was so. ¹²And the earth brought forth grass, the herb that yields seed according to its kind, and the tree that yields fruit, whose seed is in itself according to its kind. And God saw that it was good. ¹³So the evening and the morning were the third day.

¹⁴Then God said, "Let there be lights in the firmament of the heavens to divide the day from the night; and let them be for signs and seasons, and for days and years; ¹⁵and let them be for lights in the firmament of the heavens to give light on the earth"; and it was so. ¹⁶Then God made two great lights: the greater light to rule the day, and the lesser light to rule the night. He made the stars also. ¹⁷God set them in the firmament of the heavens to give light on the earth, ¹⁸and to rule over the day and over the night, and to divide the light from the darkness. And God saw that it was good. ¹⁹So the evening and the morning were the fourth day.

²⁰Then God said, "Let the waters abound with an abundance of living creatures, and let birds fly above the earth across the face of the firmament of the heavens." ²¹So God created great sea creatures and every living thing that moves, with which the waters abounded, according to their

kind, and every winged bird according to its kind. And God saw that it was good. ²²And God blessed them, saying, "Be fruitful and multiply, and fill the waters in the seas, and let birds multiply on the earth." ²³So the evening and the morning were the fifth day.

²⁴Then God said, "Let the earth bring forth the living creature according to its kind: cattle and creeping thing and beast of the earth, each according to its kind"; and it was so. ²⁵And God made the beast of the earth according to its kind, cattle according to its kind, and everything that creeps on the earth according to its kind. And God saw that it was good.

²⁶Then God said, "Let Us make man in Our image, according to Our likeness; let them have dominion over the fish of the sea, over the birds of the air, and over the cattle, over all the earth and over every creeping thing that creeps on the earth." ²⁷So God created man in His own image; in the image of God He created him; male and female He created them. ²⁸Then God blessed them, and God said to them, "Be fruitful and multiply; fill the earth and subdue it; have dominion over the fish of the sea, over the birds of the air, and over every living thing that moves on the earth."

²⁹And God said, "See, I have given you every herb that yields seed which is on the face of all the earth, and every tree whose fruit yields seed; to you it shall be for food. ³⁰Also, to every beast of the earth, to every bird of the air, and to everything that creeps on the earth, in which there is life, I have given every green herb for food"; and it was so. ³¹Then God saw everything that He had made, and indeed it was very good. So the evening and the morning were the sixth day (Genesis 1 NKJV).

¹"Thus the heavens and the earth, and all the host of them, were finished. ²And on the seventh day God ended His work which He had done, and He rested on the seventh day from all His work which He had done. ³Then God blessed the seventh day and sanctified it, because in it He rested from all His work which God had created and made. ⁴This is the history of the heavens and the earth when they were cre-

> ated, in the day that the Lord God made the earth and the heavens, ⁵before any plant of the field was in the earth and before any herb of the field had grown. For the Lord God had not caused it to rain on the earth, and there was no man to till the ground; ⁶but a mist went up from the earth and watered the whole face of the ground. ⁷And the Lord God formed man of the dust of the ground, and breathed into his nostrils the breath of life; and man became a living being" (Genesis 2:1-7 NKJV).

> ¹⁹"Out of the ground the Lord God formed every beast of the field and every bird of the air, and brought them to Adam to see what he would call them. And whatever Adam called each living creature that was its name. ²⁰So Adam gave names to all cattle, to the birds of the air, and to every beast of the field..." (Genesis 2:19-20 NKJV).

The beginning of the Bible sets the foundation for the rest of it. It establishes God as the creator of all things—*all* things. Before God intervened, there was nothing, but once He made it, He called it perfect, including mankind.

God spoke life into existence. That is the very essence of God and who He is: He makes something when there was once nothing. Although it is made plainly clear in the first two chapters of the Bible, it is actually shown throughout the entire Bible in a variety of ways.

One example of this is the idea of pregnancy. There are numerous accounts of women who were unable to bear children; however, once God intervened, they each became pregnant and gave birth to a child. In some accounts, women gave birth to multiple children. The most popular story of these women is that of Sarah, Abraham's wife. Sarah was well beyond her child-bearing years and so was her husband. Before God opened her womb, she never had children, which was considered shameful for her time. God promised Abraham that she would not only have a child but that Abraham would become the father of many nations. As you can imagine, it was difficult to believe that an elderly couple would not only conceive a child, but he would also have a generation of children to follow. That's exactly what happened, though, all because of God's miraculous hand. He not only spoke it into existence, He also created the opportunity where there was once none at all.

> "The LORD kept his word and did for Sarah exactly what he had promised. She became pregnant, and she gave birth to a son for Abraham in his old age. This happened at just the time God had said it would" (Genesis 21:1-2 NLT).

From the scripture above, you can see again that God creates or brings things—specific situations and people—into existence. God also brings forth what was once dead or dark. We see it in Genesis 1:2-3 where it says that the earth was dark and God called forth light. Take a look at it again:

> "The earth was without form, and void; and darkness was on the face of the deep. And the Spirit of God was hovering over the face of the waters. Then God said, 'Let there be light'; and there was light" (Genesis 1:2-3 NKJV).

The Bible does a great job of describing the "void" on earth. There was no life. If there was no life, there was no love or tranquility, either. No fruit (literally and figuratively) can be produced in an environment such as that. God, and only God, had to intervene in order to see something different.

Notice how the scripture says that the Spirit of God was *hovering*. God didn't just make a move impulsively. He waited for the right time to speak because as you know, everything happens in its perfect timing.

There is one more example of God bringing the dead back to life that must be added here. It's the most important of the entire Gospel and the foundation of the Christian faith.

God saw that the earth was full of sin and self-destruction. He spent the entire Old Testament of the Bible working with His chosen people to get them back to righteous living. But because they were heavily influenced by others and repeatedly fell from grace, God sent His Son, His only Son, to save them. Jesus came to this earth as a man and died on the cross as a criminal. He became the ultimate sacrifice and the ultimate example of God's love for His people, including you and me. As you go deeper in your study of the Bible, you will see how everything involved in Jesus' death and resurrection was spoken into perfect timing. Not only that, His death was necessary so that now *we* can move away from darkness and be raised to a better life—eternal life.

As I previously mentioned, it is God's very essence to bring what's dead back to life and speak into existence what was once not there. Romans 4:17, one of my favorite scriptures, says it best:

> *"That is what the Scriptures mean when God told [Abraham], 'I have made you the father of many nations.' This happened* because *Abraham believed in the God who brings the dead back to life and who creates new things out of nothing"* (Romans 4:17 NLT; emphasis added).

The same God who spoke the world into existence, who opened women's closed wombs, and who raised Jesus from the dead is the same God that lives in you and me. We are a walking miracle every single day!

The Authority within Us

Let's switch gears a little bit. Going back to the scriptures at the beginning of this chapter, I want to direct your attention to two significant things that God said to Adam and Eve. Read it again below:

> *"Then God blessed them, and God said to them, "Be fruitful and multiply; fill the earth and subdue it; <u>have dominion</u> over the fish of the sea, over the birds of the air, and over every living thing that loves on the earth"* (Genesis 1:28 NKJV; emphasis added).

> *"Out of the ground the Lord God formed every beast of the field and every buird of the field and every bird of the, and brought them to Adam to see what he would call them. <u>And whatev-</u>*

Speak Your Life into Existence

er Adam called each living creature that was its name. So Adam gave names to all cattle, to the birds of the air, and to every beast of the field..." (Genesis 2:19-20 NKJV; emphasis added).

In Genesis 1:28, God gave Adam and Eve dominion over everything surrounding them. Whatever God created, they had permission to rule over it. Has someone ever given you permission to oversee something special that you didn't originally create? It's an honorable assignment.

In Genesis 2:19-20, God took the dominion a step further. He gave Adam the task of naming all the creatures. The Bible says that whatever Adam called it, so it was. What a responsibility.

Here's the million dollar question: Why would God begin the first two chapters of the Bible by showing us how Adam and Eve had dominion over what surrounded them *and* the authority to create everlasting names just by speaking it? If we know that first impressions mean everything, why would He choose to introduce us not only to what He can create in His own power, but also to what we can do with the power we've been given? I believe God wants us to know that He has already given us authority by the power of His Spirit within us. This authority comes through the words we speak; therefore, what flows from our lips is as important as the breath in our lungs.

Just like with Adam and Eve, God has given you dominion over everything around you and has given you the authority to speak the life you want into existence. See, it is oftentimes difficult for us to grasp such an abstract concept because it is typically not what we were brought up to believe. Many of us grew in our walk with God by grasping onto the idea that God can do anything and can make anything happen, which He certainly can. In fact, He made you and me. (Again, every time we wake up to another day, we should be reminded of God's magnificent power and design.) But God didn't just create us to exist in this life. He created us to thrive and glorify His name. Well, if God created us through His infinite power, and if that same God resides within us, what can *we* also create through Him? Whatever it is, it would be an ultimate glorification of who our Creator is and what He can do.

The point that I'm making here is that we don't *have* to be consumed by our circumstances or even our emotions. God has already given us dominion over it. All we have to do is utilize what He gave us. When we're waiting on God's promises and things are not quite going the way we want it, we can sometimes feel like we are powerless, as if life is happening to us. But the opposite is actually true. The words we speak about our circumstances and desires will make all the difference to our souls, and the effects on our physical body, for that matter. Once we consistently speak it, we start to feel different. When we feel different, we then believe what we speak. Once we believe it, our world changes around us.

This would be a great time to pause and give a quick lesson on the components of our soul and how it impacts our world.

The Design of Our Soul

"Now may the God of peace make you holy in every way, and may your whole spirit and soul and body be kept blameless until our Lord Jesus Christ comes again" (1 Thessalonians 5:23 NLT).

When God created us, He designed us to have three major components: spirit, body, and soul. When we hear about each of those, we often hear them being used interchangeably, especially soul and spirit. But, God intentionally designed the spirit, soul, and body to be significant both individually and collectively. The most important point for you to know is that all three must be aligned to righteous living in order to experience the fullness of what God has already prepared for us.

According to the Word, the spirit can be defined as that which gives life to the body. James says in 2:26 that *"without the spirit, the body is dead" (NKJV).* We cannot survive without the spirit, which lives on eternally after our physical bodies return to dust.

On the other hand, our body is our outer shell and the physical parts of us that house our spirit and soul. Not only that, it is impacted by our circumstances equally as much. Think of the last time you felt nervous, angry, or even stressed. What were the physical sensations that permeated your body as a result?

The soul is the one that is often misunderstood among the three; however, it consists of your mind, will, and emotions. Whatever we think about, whatever we feel, and whatever we take action on, our soul is involved in it. Not only that, they are interconnected so that what we think about affects our feelings, and what we feel affects our actions. We can also determine the source of our thoughts, feelings, and actions by asking ourselves what we've thought about, felt, and did lately.

Now, let's go back to how this relates to what we speak. What we say (our *action*) stems from what we feel and think. If we learn to monitor our words by ensuring we speak positively, and if we train ourselves to declare the things we want, we will begin to *feel* and *think* more positively about our circumstances, even if we don't yet see God's promises come to pass. On the other hand, if we choose to speak negatively about our circumstances, we will receive what comes with that as well. Either way, we will reap what we sow as the Bible states in Proverbs 18:21: *"The tongue can bring death or life; those who love to talk will reap the consequences"* (Proverbs 18:21 NLT).

Align Yourself with God

Going back to Abraham and Sarah's story of faith, they are a clear example of what it looks like to align oneself with God. When God spoke to Abraham for the first time, promising him that he'd be the father of many nations, his name was actually Abram. Sarah's name was Sarai. As time went on in their journey towards the promise, God not only confirmed the promise, but He also changed their names.

> *"Abram fell facedown, and God said to him, "As for me, this is my covenant with you: You will be the father of many nations. No longer will you be called Abram; your name will be Abraham, for I have made you a father of many nations. I will make you very fruitful; I will make nations of you, and kings will come from you"* (Genesis 17:3-6 NIV).

> *"God also said to Abraham, "As for Sarai your wife, you are no longer*

to call her Sarai; her name will be Sarah. I will bless her and will surely give you a son by her. I will bless her so that she will be the mother of nations; kings of peoples will come from her" (Genesis 17:15-16 NIV).

God could've given them the promise in the first year that He spoke it, but He waited until the right time. For God, that time was when Abraham and Sarah were more aligned in their soul to be able to sustain the promise that was already waiting for them. They weren't ready in the first year to do that, but when God felt the time was right, He began calling them by the names that represented the promise they were preparing themselves for.

As you've read thus far and as you continue to read, the psalmist is another example after which we should model. Regardless of the apparent state of emotion he was in, and regardless of what he was dealing with, he made sure that he controlled the words that he expressed to God. He declared God's promises and referenced them often. He described his thankfulness of all God had done. Ultimately, he maximized the power of his words over his own life. In our lives, this, too, is how we should operate. The psalmist teaches us that if we are to move past this journey, we must fight our enemies—both internally and externally—with our words and declarations. As you engage in your devotion this week, make note of all the times the psalmist speaks positively about God and his situation.

So you see, making it through your journey to reach your promise is not about tangibly having a better circumstance; rather, it's about your outlook on your journey and looking forward to what's ahead. When you maintain that mindset, both of the following can be true:

1. In God's infinite power and authority, He speaks things into existence that were once non-existent.
2. By your own power and authority that God's given you, you can align your soul with His promises by speaking what you desire into existence.

Day 22

The Time is Now

Today I will

- recognize when it's time to change my posture of prayer.

Ayin

¹²¹ *Don't leave me to the mercy of my enemies,*
for I have done what is just and right.
¹²² *Please guarantee a blessing for me.*
Don't let the arrogant oppress me!
¹²³ *My eyes strain to see your rescue,*
to see the truth of your promise fulfilled.
¹²⁴ *I am your servant; deal with me in unfailing love,*
and teach me your decrees.
¹²⁵ *Give discernment to me, your servant;*
then I will understand your laws.
¹²⁶ *Lord, it is time for you to act,*
for these evil people have violated your instructions.
¹²⁷ *Truly, I love your commands*
more than gold, even the finest gold.
¹²⁸ *Each of your commandments is right.*
That is why I hate every false way.

Psalm 119:121-128 NLT

Let's Talk about It

You've spent most of these days staring at the midnight skies, wondering when your daylight will break through the darkness. You've committed to engaging in God and His words. You've done your best to walk in His ways and follow what He asks.

At this point, you could probably say that your rhythm is on beat, your worship is honest, and your love for God is pure. But you're tired of being down. You're also probably tired of the spiritual attacks, and you're ready for God to act. It may be time to now change how you pray.

We talked just a few days ago about declaring God's promises over your life as a form of healing. While that is still very much the case, you will also need to boldly declare that the enemy has no power in your life. By the very sound of Jesus' name, the enemy loses his power and has to go.

If you're going to fight against what is fighting against you, you must know that and declare it. To do this takes bold confidence and courage. That's why the time is now. You're bolder than you were before because you have God on your side.

The time is now for God to act. The enemy knows it just as much as you do. Do your part and speak it over your life, mind, body, and soul. Speak it over your life, and do your part so that God can do His.

Day 22 Devotional

Digging Deeper

The Bible says that we can place the enemy under our feet because of the name of Jesus. What do you need to declare and take back from the enemy?

_____

_____

_____

_____

_____

_____

Prayer

Dear God, thank You for being greater than what I face. In Jesus' name, darkness has no power here. Chaos has no power here. I declare a breakthrough that only You can give. I declare it through the name and blood of Jesus. Amen.

Day 23

Living to Tell about It

Today I will

- praise God for being by my side through my tough times.

- determine how to move on past my tough times.

Pe

^{129} *Your laws are wonderful.*
No wonder I obey them!
^{130} *The teaching of your word gives light,*
so even the simple can understand.
^{131} *I pant with expectation,*
longing for your commands.
^{132} *Come and show me your mercy,*
as you do for all who love your name.
^{133} *Guide my steps by your word,*
so I will not be overcome by evil.
^{134} *Ransom me from the oppression of evil people;*
then I can obey your commandments.
^{135} *Look upon me with love;*
teach me your decrees.
^{136} *Rivers of tears gush from my eyes*
because people disobey your instructions.

Psalm 119:129-136 NLT

Let's Talk about It

The first signs of a new season, particularly spring and fall, are some of the most breathtaking moments to experience. The air smells different. The birds are chirping a little more. The way the sun reflects its light differently on everything around you is undeniable.

Similarly, this is how we notice changes within ourselves, too. Things just feel "different" in the atmosphere—our atmosphere. The most noticeable difference is an unmistakable peace that fills you. It's a peace that leads you to sleep through the night and wake up rejoicing for another day. Burdens feel lifted, and you soon feel restored.

It's breathtaking to know you made it through midnight and you lived to tell about it. The moment I realized I felt different inside, I was thankful beyond measure. I spent many days thanking God that His mercies are made new every morning, and that His peace transcends any comfort or healing that the world can give.

It's important for us to thank God to acknowledge His strength and supernatural power above our own. But don't stop there. The peace feels wonderful and your perspective on your circumstance seems brand new. What are you going to do to move forward from here? How are you going to continue pursuing God?

Speaking from personal experience, it's easy to disregard everything you learn and return to old ways or habits. Prevent it!

Whether it's maintaining a set devotion schedule or changing your prayers, the point is to keep going. I assure you that God has more in store for your life.

Day 23 Devotional

Digging Deeper

Take time today to give God praise. What are you thankful for?

_____
_____
_____
_____

Not to sound pessimistic, but storms will eventually come again. You will also get through them again. Now that you've built a foundation with Him, how can you maintain your relationship with God, despite what storms may hit?

_____
_____
_____
_____

Prayer

Thank You, Lord, for what You've done in my life up to this point. I know that You have more in store for me. Please, keep guiding my steps forward. Be the lamp to my feet and show me where to move. I promise to follow. Amen.

Day 24

He won't be Mocked

Today I will

- operate as a believer in God and His word through my actions.

Tsadhe

¹³⁷ O LORD, you are righteous,
and your regulations are fair.
¹³⁸ Your laws are perfect
and completely trustworthy.
¹³⁹ I am overwhelmed with indignation,
for my enemies have disregarded your words.
¹⁴⁰ Your promises have been thoroughly tested;
that is why I love them so much.
¹⁴¹ I am insignificant and despised,
but I don't forget your commandments.
¹⁴² Your justice is eternal,
and your instructions are perfectly true.
¹⁴³ As pressure and stress bear down on me,
I find joy in your commands.
¹⁴⁴ Your laws are always right;
help me to understand them so I may live.

Psalm 119:137-144 NLT

Let's Talk about It

Typically, when we admit to trusting someone's words, we are saying we trust that person and believe they have our best interests at heart. What more does it feel like to trust God's words and promises?

- To say that we trust God means that we ultimately believe Him.
- We trust that He will fight our enemies for us.
- We are confident that He wants only the best for us.
- We believe in faith that He will never turn His back on us. He's forever faithful.

Now, we may feel this internally and may even shout it to the heavens. But the reality is that many others around us still doubt God's greatness within us.

Regardless of the opinions of others, God demands reverence and will not be mocked. As you know and have seen, His words are pure. His might is strong. When we keep that confidence in our minds and hearts, we become less and less afraid of our enemies.

Hold tightly to God's words. They're everlasting and transforming.

Day 24 Devotional

Digging Deeper

All of us are trusting God for our deepest desires. What is it that you are trusting God for at this time? Declare it and then praise Him for who He is in your life.

_____

_____

_____

_____

_____

_____

Prayer

Lord, consume me with Your presence. Comfort me with Your words. Despite the attacks and doubts being thrown at me from my enemies, I will turn to You for all my needs. You are forever faithful, and I will give You the honor You deserve. Amen.

Day 25

Pray about Everything

Today I will

- turn to God for ultimate guidance.

Qoph

¹⁴⁵ I pray with all my heart; answer me, Lord!
I will obey your decrees.
¹⁴⁶ I cry out to you; rescue me,
that I may obey your laws.
¹⁴⁷ I rise early, before the sun is up;
I cry out for help and put my hope in your words.
¹⁴⁸ I stay awake through the night,
thinking about your promise.
¹⁴⁹ In your faithful love, O Lord, hear my cry;
let me be revived by following your regulations.
¹⁵⁰ Lawless people are coming to attack me;
they live far from your instructions.
¹⁵¹ But you are near, O Lord,
and all your commands are true.
¹⁵² I have known from my earliest days
that your laws will last forever.

Psalm 119:145-152 NLT

Let's Talk about It

When I feel I am under pressure in the world, I look forward to the moment I can get home. It's my sanctuary from the storm. It's my comfort zone.

As I began to draw closer to God, I appreciated home even more because I met God there. Rather than the definition of home being the place I lay my head, it affectionately became the place I met with God.

For each of us, there must be a place where we can go to meet with God in prayer, worship, and petition. Whether you consider it your entire residence, one room, or just a small corner of a room, it should represent rest and comfort. Especially in times of distress, it becomes that place you look forward to returning. The psalmist demonstrates this truth as he petitions help from God in his most desperate moments.

In a perfect world, our problems and circumstances would go away with ease, never to return. But that's not our reality. Instead of continuing to focus on what we cannot change, we should focus on the One who can make the changes. He certainly doesn't need us in order for Him to exert His power, but He does want us to remain in alignment with Him, knowing that He is greater than anything we face and stronger than anyone who comes against us.

Meeting with Him at "home" through prayer may not change the circumstance, but it will surely bring back our peace.

Day 25 Devotional

Digging Deeper

Everyone defines home differently. For years, I struggled with what home actually meant to me. Beyond my belief, home became a completely different definition when I found it in the arms of my Savior.

Where is home for you? Ponder on that thought today and determine where you meet God most often.

_____
_____
_____
_____
_____
_____

Prayer

God, I pray that You take me to Your dwelling place—the place where I find comfort in Your arms. I've been there before, and I'm desperate without it. Thank You for always having a place for me to call home in Your arms. Amen.

Day 26

The Release

Today I will

- leave my afflictions, sadness, enemies, and burdens with God.

Resh

¹⁵³ *Look upon my suffering and rescue me,*
for I have not forgotten your instructions.
¹⁵⁴ *Argue my case; take my side!*
Protect my life as you promised.
¹⁵⁵ *The wicked are far from rescue,*
for they do not bother with your decrees.
¹⁵⁶ *LORD, how great is your mercy;*
let me be revived by following your regulations.
¹⁵⁷ *Many persecute and trouble me,*
yet I have not swerved from your laws.
¹⁵⁸ *Seeing these traitors makes me sick at heart,*
because they care nothing for your word.
¹⁵⁹ *See how I love your commandments, LORD.*
Give back my life because of your unfailing love.
¹⁶⁰ *The very essence of your words is truth;*
all your just regulations will stand forever.

Psalm 119:153-160 NLT

Let's Talk about It

The more you know God, the easier it becomes to stabilize your emotions. Throughout this devotional, the psalmist is our near-perfect example of how our emotions are up one day and down the next, especially during our most difficult seasons.

The world teaches us to operate from our emotions and react according to what we feel. Here are some examples:

- We should retaliate when we've been wronged.
- We should handle all things ourselves and with our own might.
- It is up to us to figure it all out with our own wisdom.

What did you notice about the psalmist all this time? Although his emotions were unstable, his unrelenting love and devotion toward God were always consistent. While his emotions often made him feel like he was on the verge of death, he continuously looked to God for life. His prayer in today's reading is no different.

Dear ones, it really does get easier as you draw closer to God. As you come to know Him, you receive the fruit of the Spirit: love, joy, peace, patience, kindness, goodness, faithfulness, gentleness and self-control (Galatians 5:22-23 NKJV).

Notice that the fruit of the Spirit does not include fear. God's Spirit doesn't give that, which means it's not from Him. For that reason, there is no more need to embrace the fear that has clouded your darkness. Instead, give it to God. There's no need for bitterness. Again, that's a burden God can take on.

Remove those burdens that have been holding you down. Tell them they're no longer welcome. Then, look to God for a renewed spirit and fresh faith. That's how you stabilize your emotions.

Day 26 Devotional

Digging Deeper

There are certain emotions that, if left uncontrolled, will completely take away what God is trying to do in your life. What emotions do you need to control? Make it a point to write them down, and then give them to God. After all, that's what He sent His Son to die on the cross for.

_____

_____

_____

_____

_____

_____

Prayer

God, I'm leaving my burdens with You. I thank You for being able to do all things I cannot, and I pray that you stabilize my emotions so that I can focus on You and not my circumstances. Amen.

Day 27 and 28
Recap and Reflection

Psalm 119:121-160

Go back through this week's reading. Write down any new thoughts that come to mind to deepen your perspective and reflection that you've gained.

_____
_____
_____
_____

Digging Deeper

Is there something you need to dig deeper on this weekend? Explore the things you wrote down this week and see if more revelations come to mind.

_____
_____
_____
_____

Prayer

After going back through this week's readings, write a personal prayer to God. Thank Him for what He's done for you and confess to Him what you've been holding onto this week. Release it into His hands through your prayer.

_____

_____

_____

_____

_____

For Such a Time as This

We are nearing the end of our journey in this book while studying Psalm 119. We've certainly come a long way in almost thirty days. Let's do another recap:

- We've discussed the importance of a spiritual realignment with God in order to awaken our senses and draw closer to Him.
- We realized that only God can meet our deepest needs, and supplementing other people and things will never last.
- We uncovered the differences between what the world defines as love and what God originally designed love to be.
- We learned how serving others is a two-edged sword in that it brings blessings to other people and also ignites God's healing in our own lives.
- We understood the necessity of getting plain old honest with God in a way that releases us from

holding onto baggage or burdens while giving us room to breathe in His works.
- Lastly, we were reminded of the God-given power to speak what we want into existence in order to align with what God is bringing us into.

Overall, my hope for you throughout this book was to grasp the understanding that while we wait on God's promises, we have work to do. We cannot simply sit with our hands out, palms facing upward, and wait for something to drop from the sky. Don't get me wrong, God can surely drop something from the sky if He so pleased, but would we appreciate that blessing as much if all we had to do was receive with no additional effort given on our parts?

One way I like to think of this is through an idea of receiving a promotion. If I walked into work one day and my boss said she would give me a 25% pay raise for no reason other than that she liked me, I would be happy—ecstatic even. But if I worked hard for a year by going the extra mile and increasing my results because I had goals of being promoted, I would appreciate it much more when my boss came to me afterward and told me that I've *earned* promotion. I would know instantly that I worked hard for it. I would know that it came from effort, not idle expectation for it to just be handed to me.

That's the reason for our midnight experience. It's the time that God places us on a journey to be more aligned to Him. As you've probably endured, your midnight experience can be some of the most difficult moments of your life filled with overwhelming emotion and uncertainty. A midnight experience has the potential to pull at your deepest fears, strongholds, and especially your faith.

At the same time, your midnight experience may be the closest you've ever felt to God. During my own experience, my faith was tested repeatedly, but it was also increasing because of all the ways God revealed to me that He was carrying me through this journey. I wasn't alone, and neither are you.

One of the clearest examples from the Bible is through the story of the Apostle Paul in the New Testament. He, too, had a midnight experience. But once he became more aligned to God, he received a promise that he couldn't have dreamed up on his own. Let's go deeper into his story.

Paul's Midnight Experience

Paul's original name was Saul. Before his figurative midnight experience occurred, he was one of the biggest enemies of the Christian church at the time. His goal was to make the whole Christian movement extinct because it did not fit with the traditional Jewish tradition.

His methods were ravaging. He ordered people to be killed simply because of who they were and what they believed. (It doesn't sound too far off from what is occurring in the world today.) The root of Saul's motivation was pride. He believed that because he was such an advocate for the Jewish tradition and religion, no one or nothing else mattered. Take a look at how Paul, once transformed, described his former life.

> "I am a Jew, born in Tarsus of Cilicia, but brought up in this city. I studied under Gamaliel and was thoroughly trained in the law of our ancestors. I was just as zealous for God as any of you are today. I persecuted the followers of this Way to their death, arresting both men and women and throwing them into prison, as the high priest and all the Council can themselves testify. I even obtained letters from them to their associates in Damascus, and went there to bring these people as prisoners to Jerusalem to be punished" (Acts 22:3-5 NIV).

Within that same conversation, Paul talked about the moment God completely changed his life by calling him out from the path he was on.

> "Then [Ananias] said: 'The God of our ancestors has chosen you to know his will and to see the Righteous One and to hear words from his mouth. You will be his witness to all people of what you have seen and

heard. And now what are you waiting for? Get up, be baptized and wash your sins away, calling on his name'" (Acts 22:14-16 NIV).

It must have been overwhelming to hear that the same God you've been persecuting now wants to use *you* for His glory. Paul couldn't just go into ministry the next day; he had to be trained by other apostles, baptized and transformed. For him, it was a process that required him to draw closer to God in order to align to what He was calling him to do.

God placed a promise on Paul's heart—a promise that He would be used to build the Church. Having written most of the New Testament books of the Bible, we see that this promise was fulfilled; however, it started with humble beginnings of training, alignment, and simply knowing Jesus.

Like Paul, we also have to start with humble beginnings of learning and growing. You may be in a position now where you are wondering when and how your promises will be fulfilled, especially if God has already spoken them to you for a future time. One thing I've come to understand is that God will not give us a promise right away. If He did, we wouldn't be able to sustain it. God loves us so much that He takes time to work with us as we learn to align our mind, will, and emotions to His.

Yes, God has a mind, will, and emotions, too. His thoughts (mind) are higher than ours. His ways (will) are not our ways. He loves (emotions) greater than we could ever love, and He demonstrated that by sending His Son to die for our sins. Therefore, if He's going to bless us for the greater purpose of using us to demonstrate His glory, we must be aligned to Him as much as we can. Think about it: What kinds of contradictions would come of us thinking and behaving like a heathen but claiming to represent God? Enough said.

It's important to understand that God is not expecting us to be perfect by any means. In fact, no human was ever perfect other than Jesus Christ. God is, however, expecting us to be transformed by the renewing of our minds, which will cause us to think differently, feel differently, and act differently in ways that consciously represent the God we serve; and, if we find ourselves outside of His will, we have the strength and moral compass to get back on track.

While we wait on God to move, we must understand that God is waiting on us to move as well—to move closer to Him. Again, it doesn't happen overnight. It's a process. In fact, it's a similar process to metal being refined and purified. While it does take time, and that time may feel like it's longer than necessary, it is surely worth it.

As we near the end of this book, continue to take time to reflect on your journey. Whether you're still at the beginning stages of your journey or you have been through this for a while now, it's necessary for you to take inventory of where you've been and where God is taking you—similar to the way I did it at the beginning of this recap section. While we're in the middle of our midnight experience, it's really easy to take ourselves above our circumstances to understand that God has a perfect plan. Prior to this journey, He already prepared you for such a time as this. You possess within you everything you need to get through this time, whether that be resources, friends, patience, or time. He's prepared you, and He will sustain you. All He needs now is for you to recognize it and align to it.

Section Five

Day Twenty-Nine through Day Thirty

Conclusion, but Not the End

I would love to tell you that your midnight experience will come to an end the moment you finish the last word in this book. I would love to tell you that you have successfully completed your journey and have been promoted to the next level of blessings. Unfortunately, I choose not to conclude with that false hope.

If it was as easy as going through a 30-day "program" just to receive the promises of God and move out of the difficult moments in our life, then would we really need Him? Allowing ourselves to believe that a how-to manual can solve our problems would inadvertently imply that we cannot only do this thing called life ourselves, but we can also get the glory for it.

This is why God's thoughts are not our thoughts, and His ways are not our ways. God knows that if He gave supernatural permission for blessings to move on our human timeline, we wouldn't fully appreciate what all goes into God bringing a blessing to pass. We think we would. We may even convince ourselves that we would, but we wouldn't. For that reason, we must trust God's timeline and plans for our life. His ways are perfect, so He knows the perfect time to release a promise to us. I speak from personal experience when I tell you that His perfect timing is always better than what we could imagine. King Solomon said it best in Proverbs: *"You can make many plans, but the LORD's purpose will prevail"* (Proverbs 19:21 NLT).

The ultimate purpose of this book is a three-fold: To acknowledge what many believers face in the dark moments, to encourage believers to persist through those times of waiting and wondering, and to guide believers in redirecting the focus away from what they see and onto God. Let me break those down further.

Acknowledgment

I recognize that it is sometimes difficult to reveal what's really happening within us behind the guise of a smile. Sometimes it can feel unholy to have real questions for God or possess real pain within, regardless of why that emotional pain is there. As a result, many Christians find themselves suffering in silence. It's time to bring it to the forefront. We as believers need to know that it's completely normal and natural to struggle at times with understanding the God we serve. When channeled correctly, we learn that it actually draws us closer to God rather than separates us.

Encouragement

How can our personal struggles draw us closer to God? You may be wondering. When we face struggles for an extended period of time, we eventually empty ourselves from our natural resources to cope. That time period is different for each of us, but it all leads us to the same point of desperation for God's strength over our own. What I've found to be true in my own life is that it is during those times that I hear Him the most. It's not that He wasn't speaking before; rather, it's that I am more cognizant. The same is true for anyone who is seeking God during the storms. Before we reach the point of saying, "God, You're the only One who can fix this situation," we are spending time trying to figure it out on our own. It's a waste of time and energy. Therefore, be encouraged knowing that God is waiting for you to draw near to Him. He's our ultimate comforter, and His presence will indeed encourage us to press on.

Guidance

Once you feel acknowledged and encouraged, you're likely going to desire a next step to move forward. God's words are intended to be the lamp to our feet that guides us from step to step and to another step. But because the Bible usually doesn't always spell out exactly what we should do in our specific situation, we must trust the Holy Spirit to do that work for us. Regardless of what we're exposed to (the Bible, a faith-based book, a sermon, or a friend's helpful words), the Holy Spirit can pinpoint exactly what we need to hear and place it in our hearts. When this happens, we are able to redirect our focus back to God rather than anything we endure. Perhaps this enlightenment and redirection occurred at several points during these thirty days.

The Journey doesn't Stop Here

When I first read the last two sections of Psalm 119, I felt incomplete. I wondered why there wasn't a more traditional conclusion that summarized everything we read in such a long body of work. I was expecting somewhat of a happy ending. I was expecting something to indicate all things would be better now and I'd see a rainbow outside my window the following day. But that expectation came through the natural eyes from which I was looking. When I looked through my spiritual eyes, I could then see that verses 161-176 possess the perfect ending to what we've read. Not only that, God knew we needed to hear those specific words.

In our last two devotions, you'll see that the psalmist's tone is different than when he started in verse 1. While it appears that he is still facing struggles, he remains focused on God's word and seems to find peace from knowing that God is with him. In fact, in verses 166-168, the psalmist acknowledges all the things he has done during these troublesome times, letting us know he has resolved

The Midnight Experience

that God's will is the only thing that matters to him now, not the enemies or the chaos.

On Day 30, you'll see a sharp turn of tone and emotion, though. The psalmist reverts back to more requests from God, begging to be rescued from what he's facing. *I thought he was at peace about what was happening around him,* you may still wonder. While he may be at peace in who his God is, the storms are still raging. His candid switch in emotion here demonstrates the truest depiction of what it means to be a believer in this world: Through the raging storms, I know and believe in the God who saves.

As a Christian, it would be lovely to reach a point where we can say, "I have arrived!" But we know that's not how Christianity works. Our ultimate arrival is to make it to heaven for all eternity. God doesn't expect us to arrive because that would indicate perfection. He does expect us to draw closer to Him throughout our various seasons. The closer the relationship with God, the faster we'll be able to obtain peace during the storms.

My best advice for you is to keep going because it doesn't stop at the turn of the final page. Resource your life so that you can continue to learn about the character of God. In your obedience and devotion to Him, He'll reveal more and more of His will for your life right now and in the future. Remember, it's a step-by-step process. And when you finally do attain the promises of God that you've longed for, you'll appreciate it much more because you'll understand why you had to go through all that you did to be ready for them.

Day 29

Truly Transformed Forever

Today I will

- identify how obeying God has sustained me.

Shin

¹⁶¹ *Powerful people harass me without cause,*
but my heart trembles only at your word.
¹⁶² *I rejoice in your word*
like one who discovers a great treasure.
¹⁶³ *I hate and abhor all falsehood,*
but I love your instructions.
¹⁶⁴ *I will praise you seven times a day*
because all your regulations are just.
¹⁶⁵ *Those who love your instructions have great peace*
and do not stumble.
¹⁶⁶ *I long for your rescue, LORD,*
so I have obeyed your commands.
¹⁶⁷ *I have obeyed your laws,*
for I love them very much.
¹⁶⁸ *Yes, I obey your commandments and laws*
because you know everything I do.

Psalm 119:161-168 NLT

Let's Talk about It

"How do you know you know?" That's a question I often get when I tell them I've been changed. To be honest, I don't know how I know. I just do.

Most people don't know what occurs during your midnight experience; therefore, they surely wouldn't understand what your transformation means to you. They aren't aware of the conversations you've had with God, asking, "How much longer do I have to go through this?" or "Why am I feeling this way, God?" They didn't see the tears that flowed from your eyes out of pure fatigue from all that you're facing.

But God knows. Thank God for His comforting words. Thank God for His strength that carries you through the night.

When you read the psalmist's reflections today, it is apparent that he is transformed:

- His focus is not on his enemies, but on God's words (v. 161).
- His desires are more aligned to that of God (v. 163).
- The amount of time he spends with God has increased to seven times per day (v. 164).

He recognizes the different types of emotional stability of those who abide by His words and those who don't (v. 165).

In the psalmist's circumstance, it doesn't matter what other people see different in him, it is more important that he sees it within himself. The same should be true for us. While the world may still think of you as the same person, just know one important thing: God is transforming you from the inside out through your commitment to Him and His words.

As you go through your day, continue to praise God for the small changes you see in your life. Acknowledge His presence and His ability to stabilize you. After all, unlike the world's transformation, God's transformation lasts for eternity.

Day 29 Devotional

Digging Deeper

Change doesn't always come like a flash of lightning, making itself so apparent in your life. Many times, it is subtle. You wake up one day and realize that you are just different.

What changes have you noticed within yourself? Think about all the ways you've seen changes within your attitude, emotions, thought-process, and even your circumstances. Write it down in an act of gratitude.

_____

_____

_____

_____

_____

_____

Prayer

Dear God, I'm in total awe of You. Thank you for sustaining me all this time. There is no one like You. Thank You for closing doors that no one can open and opening doors that no one can close. You are my God- now and forever. Amen.

Day 30

Total Dependence on God

Today I will

- recognize what it looks like to have complete surrender to God.

Taw

[169] O Lord, listen to my cry;
give me the discerning mind you promised.
[170] Listen to my prayer;
rescue me as you promised.
[171] Let praise flow from my lips,
for you have taught me your decrees.
[172] Let my tongue sing about your word,
for all your commands are right.
[173] Give me a helping hand,
for I have chosen to follow your commandments.
[174] O Lord, I have longed for your rescue,
and your instructions are my delight.
[175] Let me live so I can praise you,
and may your regulations help me.
[176] I have wandered away like a lost sheep;
come and find me,
for I have not forgotten your commands.

Psalm 119:169-176 NLT

Let's Talk about It

"Trust in the Lord with all your heart; do not depend on your own understanding. Seek his will in all you do and he will show you which path to take" (Proverbs 3:5-6 NLT).

This section of Psalm 119 is the perfect conclusion for this devotional. The fact that the psalmist petitions almost a dozen times proves his humble surrender to God's plan for his life versus his own plan. Possessing a character such as this means that pride is removed, selfishness is filtered through grace, and control is relinquished.

From midnight to the breaking of dawn, there is a peace in knowing that God is within you. He's near, and He has always been near. His love is eternally faithful and His words prove that He will continue to provide for us as long as we lay down our life for Him.

"If you try to hang on to your life, you will lose it. But if you give up your life for my sake, you will save it." (Matthew 16:25 NLT).

Day 30 Devotional

Digging Deeper

On your final day of the devotion, take time to thank God for not only where you are now, but where you've been. His word says that He works out everything for His purpose; therefore, all things, including this one, will grow you. You'll never be defeated, and the enemy has no power over you. Thank God for making that a reality for you, in Jesus' name.

_____
_____
_____
_____
_____
_____

Prayer

Dear God, I worship You because of who You are, not because of what You can do for me. Wherever You go, I will follow. Thank You for always pursuing me, especially on this journey. I will forever be Yours. Amen.

Closing Thoughts

"Biblically, waiting is not just something we have to do until we get what we want. Waiting is part of the process of becoming what God wants us to be."

John Ortberg[5]

We've heard it said plenty of times that patience is a virtue. Regardless of who we are or where we come from, we are required to learn what it actually means to wait on what we can't have yet. Even from the time babies are able to desire something, they must also learn the tough lesson of how to not act their worst when they can't have the item at that moment.

Subconsciously, we are aware that waiting will be to our benefit in our daily walk with God, though, it is quite painful to live out — so painful that we find ourselves in some really dark places.

The need to wait on God rather than making things happen on our own is what fuels the midnight experience. Do you know about clouds that blanket the evening sky of our experience?

The Midnight Experience

They're filled with our impatience. The wind that blows around us echoes the battle cry between our plans versus God's. Even if no one else knows what or why we're *really* suffering in this season, we know deep down that it's because we want to rule on the throne.

The throne? That's a term that we usually hear about in fairy tales. What we're confident about is that the one who sits on the throne is the one who makes the decisions. The same is true for God's throne. It's not us who sits on the throne. It's Him; therefore, He alone decides when to move, how to move, and what to move on.

So, is all of this about waiting? You ask. Yes and no. The thing that brings us closer to God is by walking in obedience to all the things He calls us to do. This, in return, brings glory to Him and a sense of purpose to us. Until we willingly lay our lives down to His desires above our own, we won't ever be satisfied.

Pastor John Ortberg says it best in the quote above. Our end goal should not be to get what we want. (If the prize is our primary focus, then we are disregarding the One who gives the prize.) Instead, our end goal should be about becoming more of the person God wants us to be. His plans will always be greater than our plans. The promises that we receive at the end of our obedience will be greater than we could ever dream up on our own.

Your waiting is all about your pursuit of God. That is what it's all about. To understand His love and His plans for you takes time and patience; if He unraveled it all at once, we wouldn't be able to handle all the ways He intricately loves us.

As you wait on God, wait with great expectation knowing that He's working things out even when you cannot see it with your natural eyes. You are exactly where He wants you and He will lead you on where to go next. Be thankful that you don't have to carry the burden of planning out your life and achieving your own promises. You have a King who is doing it for you.

Peace,

Elana

Notes

1. *A Knock at Midnight*; King Jr, Carson, & Holloran, 2000

2. Bondage. (n.d.). Accessed July 26, 2018, from https://www.merriam-webster.com/dictionary/bondage

3. Evans, J. (2012). MarriageToday: *Our Deepest Needs.* Accessed on July 26, 2018, from https://www.youtube.com/watch?v=A-DgRK2u7zM

4. Jeanty, J. (2018). *Why is the Eye of the Storm so Calm?* Accessed July 26, 2018 through https://sciencing.com/eye-hurricane-calm-6365963.html

5. Pinsky, R. (2000). *Americans' favorite poems: the Favorite Poem Project anthology.* (First Edition). New York: W.W. Norton.

6. Ortberg, J (2016). *Learning to Wait.* Accessed July 26, 2018 through https://www.faithgateway.com/learning-to-wait/#.W4JzYehKjIU

About the Author

Elana Cole is a lover of education. She began her career in 2005 as a teacher to 131 inner city high school students. That work brought her to a humble understanding of the importance of expanding one's mind and transforming one's potential. Through her career, she has realized her life mission to teach and develop others to be the best versions of themselves both within the church and within today's culture.

Elana currently lives in Memphis, Tennessee and works as a professional coach and mentor to new teachers. From her years of experience, spiritual guidance, and passion for seeing changed lives, she has fostered confidence and leadership to hundreds of educators across the city.

When she is not coaching or training, she enjoys yoga, traveling, and snuggling up to a good book. She also devotes herself to building up her local church through serving, teaching, and spreading God's word on international missions.

You can find Elana regularly writing on her blog *Empowered Narrative* at www.empowerednarrative.com, which teaches others how to transform the way they live and love through the love of God.

www.ingramcontent.com/pod-product-compliance
Lightning Source LLC
Chambersburg PA
CBHW032037290426
44110CB00012B/844